D1230199

# Journalism Standards of Work Today

# Journalism Standards of Work Today:

*Using History to Create a New Code of Journalism Ethics*

By

Stephen A. Banning

**Cambridge**
**Scholars**
Publishing

Journalism Standards of Work Today:
Using History to Create a New Code of Journalism Ethics

By Stephen A. Banning

This book first published 2020

Cambridge Scholars Publishing

Lady Stephenson Library, Newcastle upon Tyne, NE6 2PA, UK

British Library Cataloguing in Publication Data
A catalogue record for this book is available from the British Library

ISBN (10): 1-5275-5803-7
ISBN (13): 978-1-5275-5803-8

# TABLE OF CONTENTS

# CHAPTER ONE

# DÉJÀ VU IN MODERN MEDIA

This book is a guide to understanding not only the nature of traditional journalism codes of ethics, but why they were introduced and the problems they were created to address. This will serve as a practical guide for the journalist navigating in today's communication environment in that, more than just a description of ethics, it is a manual for understanding modern journalism challenges. The author uses history as a roadmap exhibiting the way technology has triggered ethical journalism challenges in the past, and how the same template utilized by past journalists can provide a framework for establishing modern communication values. While some of the concepts are sophisticated, the language used to explain them is understandable, and easy to comprehend examples from recent cases are used to break down concepts in clear, simple, terms. The author will outline both past ethical shortcomings and a new code of ethics based on past journalistic standards of work and current responsibilities. Discussion questions will be included at the end of each chapter to encourage engagement through critical scaffolding, beginning with identification items and moving toward topics requiring critical thinking.

This book will reveal the similarity between current content purveyors pioneering todays' communication frontier and journalists during the First Industrial Revolution who struggled with occupational identity and mores as the scope of information dissemination exponentially expanded. Through the lens of past journalism successes and failures, this book provides insights into journalists' roles and standards of work in the context of technologically fueled cultural shifts. The reader will find that current challenges posed by technological transformations have been examined before, and while the answers may apply to different delivery channels, the bedrock principles remain unchanged. The reader will be challenged to balance society's needs with journalistic responsibilities in regard to setting standards in the modern times.

The reader will consider the components of ethical journalism and who modern journalists are. Additionally, this book examines early journalists who tackled questions on journalism's societal value, standards of work, organizations and education. As in modern times, journalists in the First Industrial Revolution faced monumental changes from improved printing technology that increased information dissemination, resultant in a transformation of audiences caused by historically rising literacy rates.[1]

Organizations formed to surmount these challenges, becoming crucial to developing ethical norms in journalism. The reader will be encouraged to consider if these norms still exist, apply and serve society. The prescription is that modern journalism consumers and journalists need to discuss critical questions regarding technology, with the emphasis not just on how technology might be used, but about responsibilities journalists incur and the standards to which they should aspire. However, the underlying values that prevailed when the Canons of Journalism were created a century ago will be found to be the same as those required in modern times, applied to new technological contexts.

It may seem strange that news dissemination was originally based on a rudimentary printing press, as the challenges of modern technology extend far beyond those posed by the limited hand operated presses of the late 1700s. At that time, freedom of the press was limited to those who could afford a relatively expensive printing press. Today, journalists go by many titles, and while some vloggers, bloggers, micro-bloggers, podcast hosts and Facebook posters perform many functions of the traditional journalist, many would never think of calling themselves journalists. Despite this, what has been called the non-traditional media has long ago surpassed the traditional media in terms of news dissemination, and even social media messages intended for a few may quickly reach tens of millions.

While prevailing challenges in modern times stem from the Third Industrial Revolution rather than the First Industrial Revolution, the same questions remain as to responsible journalisms' place and value. This book reveals how early publishers considered these questions, assembled to gather opinions and formed the basis of codes of ethics over many decades prior to

---

[1] Jim A. Kuypers, *Partisan Journalism: A History of Media Bias in the United States* (New York: Rowman & Littlefield Publishers, 2013), 16.

the principles inspiring the Canons of Journalism in the early twentieth century. It is these lessons on which enduring values can be distilled.[2]

## From One Technological Revolution to the Next

This current chapter discusses the premise of this book and its purpose as well as offering a brief overview of the chapters that lie ahead. It began by discussing how this book builds toward a new proposed code of ethics in the Digital Age, setting the stage by looking at how the First Industrial Revolution began and changed both technology and culture.

Chapter Two will describe how the First Industrial Revolution fueled changes in media information gathering, production, content and dissemination that resulted in a loss of credibility, which in turn made a case for a code of ethics. There were also many changes in culture in the first half of the nineteenth century, as the Industrial Revolution radically transformed society, the media being no exception. One of the greatest changes occurred in the 1830s, when the Penny Press Era ushered in innovations still used today. Because of its continuing impact and its effect on journalism ethics the Penny Press will be closely examined.[3]

The Penny Press newspapers were known for sensational stories and lurid headlines which troubled some publishers who became concerned that the new mass-produced news was tainting society and causing all newspapers to lose credibility.[4] Another challenge created by the Penny Press system was newspaper advertising of patent medicines, the sometimes dangerous and usually dubious healing potions that heavily supported many newspapers. Because there was no government regulation of pharmaceuticals, patent medicines often contained substances not mentioned on the label including heroin and cocaine, causing death from overdoses even among children. Both of these problems, sensationalism and conflicts of interest, resulted in a loss of newspaper credibility.[5]

---

[2] Stephen A. Banning, "Truth is Our Ultimate Goal," *American Journalism* 16, no. 1 (Winter 1999): 17.

[3] Michael Schudson, *Discovering the News: A Social History of American Newspapers* (New York: Basic Books, 1981), 57.

[4] David B. Sachsman and David W. Bulla, eds., *Sensationalism: Murder, Mayhem, Mudslinging, Scandals, and Disasters in 19th Century Reporting* (Piscataway, NJ: Transaction Publishers, 2013), xxi.

[5] Dan King, *Quackery Unmasked* (New York: D. Clapp, 1858), 295.

Chapter Three will consider how the concept of professionalization influenced journalism culture, an important historical component to consider as we examine it as an early catalyst for journalism ethics, exemplifying journalists' answers to questions elicited by the newly created mass media. During the First Industrial Revolution, three occupations (doctors, lawyers and the clergy) had risen in status and were called professions, being seen as the expert class of individuals needed in an industrialized society.[6] As a result, some journalists wanted to professionalize to keep newspapers from losing more credibility, and thus, professionalization was seen as a way for journalists to ethically respond to the new mass communication challenges.[7]

There were several criteria for an occupation to become a profession which included professional associations, university education, a code of ethics and sometimes licensing.[8] Unfortunately, journalism was a poor candidate for full professionalization in that not all of the tenets of professionalization reflected journalism's unique case. The tenets of professionalism set by doctors, lawyers and the clergy were associations, codes of ethics, university education, licensing and autonomy. While journalists in the nineteenth century formed associations, codes of ethics and advocated for university education, licensing was anathema to the concept of a free press and was never seriously deliberated. Still, many journalists identified as professionals in the nineteenth century and even more so in the twentieth, with the establishment of university journalism schools, professional associations and codes of ethics.[9]

During the second half of the nineteenth century, many associations of editors and publishers had been formed, some specifically as professional organizations where discussions of ethics and university education began.[10] From these humble beginnings, the elements of professionalization were formulated into implementable actions at the start of the twentieth century

---

[6] Howard M. Vollmer and Donald L. Mills, *Professionalization* (Englewood Cliffs, NJ: Prentice-Hall Inc., 1966), 2; Magali Sarfatti Larson, *The Rise of Professionalism: A Sociological Analysis* (Berkeley, CA: University of California Press, 1977), 6.
[7] Stephen A. Banning "The Professionalization of Journalism: A Nineteenth-Century Beginning," *Journalism History* 24, no. 4 (Winter 1998-1999): 158.
[8] Philip Elliott, *The Sociology of the Professions* (New York: Herder and Herder, 1973), 40.
[9] Banning, "The Professionalization of Journalism," 158.
[10] Stephen A. Banning, "Press Clubs Champion Journalism Education," in *Journalism 1908: Birth of a Profession,* ed. Betty Winfield (Columbia, MO: University of Missouri Press, 2008), 65.

when the first school of journalism commenced at the University of Missouri and another shortly thereafter at Columbia University.[11]

Chapter Four delves into the content of the first nationally recognized press codes of ethics, which form the basis of current ethical discussions. The first widely adopted journalism codes of ethics came in the early twentieth century shortly after the foundation of the first university schools of journalism (at the University of Missouri and Columbia University) and the beginning of the two professional press clubs (American Society of Newspaper Editors and Sigma Delta Chi). The codes of ethics were similar to each other and borrowed from ethical discussions that had started more than half a century before, but unlike previous ethical discussions and loose codes of journalism ethics, the American Society of Newspaper Editors and Sigma Delta Chi codes became widely accepted and implemented.[12] These codes addressed issues journalists had discussed in press associations for half a century.

The American Society of Newspaper Editors code of ethics was called the Canons of Journalism and emphasized seven topics: 1) responsibility, 2) freedom of the press, 3) independence, 4) sincerity, truthfulness, accuracy, 5) impartiality, 6) fair play and 7) decency. These seven elements addressed challenges which had emerged over the previous century. The ideas behind these elements are discussed in Chapters Five through Eight as a touchstone for understanding journalism values.[13]

Chapter Five will examine the two items of responsibility and independence from the Canons of Journalism in relation to current communication conditions in the Digital Age, in order to ascertain if these ethical elements are still relevant almost a century after they was codified. These elements directly relate to conflicts of interest challenges, which occur when a journalist is influenced by a latent factor.[14] For example, a reporter who recommends a product would have a conflict of interest if he or she had been paid secretly by the product's manufacture. Even though a reporter might openly inform an audience that he or she had been given an incentive,

---

[11] Banning, "Press Clubs Champion Journalism Education," 65.

[12] Banning, "Truth is Our Ultimate Goal," 17.

[13] Charles L. Allen, *Canons of Journalism, Adopted by the American Society of Newspaper Editors in Convention 1925* [sic] (Urbana, IL: University of Illinois Studio Press, 1928), 1.

[14] Michael Davis and Andrew Stark, *Conflict of Interest in the Professions* (New York: Oxford University Press, 2001), 78.

it could still be considered a conflict of interest, in the same way a trial judge would be considered to have a conflict of interest if he or she accepted a bribe from a defendant. The reader is asked to consider if this is an ethical element which should still be considered today. Factors damaging to journalism independence historically are discussed including deregulation, concentration of ownership, excessive government regulation, relationships and advertisers.

Chapter Six looks at the Canons of Journalism elements of sincerity, truthfulness and accuracy (which the Canons of Journalism considers one element), and impartiality, which can be related to current challenges of "fake news." While the "fake news" label is new, the accusation is old and one of the reasons codes of ethics were created in the first place. In times past, fabricated stories were called hoaxes.[15] Even though many information sources are truthful, the 2016 United States presidential election revealed the digital landscape allows misinformation to circulate easily, especially through mediums such as Twitter and Facebook where some political reports were complete fabrications.[16]

Chapter Seven studies the Canons of Journalism elements of fair play and decency which encompass the current ethical challenges of privacy, sensationalism and gatekeeping. The chapter looks at whether these concerns are damaging to society today and if they belong in a new code of ethics.

According to the Canons of Journalism, fair play involves respecting privacy and correcting mistakes. Among other areas, this speaks to the current online problem of "doxing," exposing a person's name and address against his or her wishes. The difficulty of sensationalism is embodied in the current practice of digital information producers who use click-bait. This principle is dealt with in the Canons of Journalism.[17]

Chapter Eight examines current journalism challenges in relation to the construction of a new code of ethics. Many journalists after the First Industrial Revolution saw a need for a code of ethics, a belief that resulted in widely used codes in the twentieth century. Today, at a time when traditional media sources have declined, media critics are challenging the

---

[15] Matthew Goodman, *The Sun and the Moon* (New York: Basic Books, 2008), 147.
[16] Jesus Velasco, *American Presidential Elections in a Comparative Perspective: The World is Watching* (Lanham, MD: Rowman and Littlefield, 2019), 14.
[17] Paul Alfred Pratte, *Gods Within the Machine: A History of the American Society of Newspaper Editors, 1923-1993* (Westport, CT: Praeger, 1995), 205-6.

credibility of many kinds of information.[18] Consequently, Chapter Eight synthesizes information from previous chapters to propose a new code of ethics. Based on earlier discussion, three enduring foundations of journalism emerge, and a code of ethics is constructed with similarity to the Canons of Journalism where old and new concerns intersect.

## The First Industrial Revolution

This section begins an examination of the First Industrial Revolution that propelled mass media into existence. This time period is examined because it goes to the center of the purpose of this book, that is to compare early journalism problems and solutions with the modern day problems, in order to see if past standards of work, specifically those culminating in the Canons of Journalism, can provide elements for a modern code of ethics.

The First Industrial Revolution in the United States took place at the end of the eighteenth century and can be described as an agrarian economy shifting to one mechanized in character, a sea change that greatly impacted society. Historians often refer to this period as the First Industrial Revolution, paying deference to two additional later periods of industrial growth. The time period was fueled by inventions, which required factories for production and transportation for distribution. These ripples in society inspired a migration to urban areas and new transportation routes between cities. As a result, the time it took materials to be manufactured was exponentially reduced, permitting those who owned the means of production to reap the benefits of an economy of scale, and because of the increased per capita production, society achieved a higher standard of living.[19]

One of the inventions that helped start the First Industrial Revolution in the United States was textile milling technology, based on an English device introduced by Samuel Slater in 1790. Historians generally agree that the First United States Industrial Revolution continued from this time until the 1830s.[20] In order for society to take advantage of industrial innovation, new ways of working had to be introduced. The first work technique, called the

---

[18] Aviv Ovadya, "What is Credibility Made of," *Columbia Journalism Review*, March 21, 2019, https://www.cjr.org/tow_center_reports/ovadya-credibility-journalism-ocasio.php

[19] Robert E. Lucas, Jr., *Lectures on Economic Growth* (Cambridge, MA.: Harvard University Press, 2002), 109.

[20] Christopher Simonds, *Samuel Slater's Mill and the Industrial Revolution* (Englewood Cliffs, NJ: Silver Burdett Press, 1990), 19.

outwork system, was a method whereby parts of the manufacturing process were accomplished in separate homes. However, a more efficient method, called the factory system, was later adopted, which allowed all the work to be done in one place, often by large assemblies of workers. Soon textile mill towns were constructed on the East Coast of the United States, the most famous of which was in Lowell, Massachusetts, where young women were recruited to run the machines.[21]

Successfully harnessing steam was important for the First Industrial Revolution because it helped power both factories for manufacturing and transportation for distributing. Steam power has been used in some form for over two thousand years, but it took a series of inventions to create steam machines that would change the world of manufacturing. Without the power of steam, it is difficult to imagine mass communication taking place, and therefore, a brief look at the development of this important technology will help set the stage for a discussion of mass communication.[22]

While a Roman engineer known as the Hero of Alexandria is credited with creating or at least first describing a steam device known as the Aeolipile in the first century, it was not until the late seventeenth century that significant improvements moved it past the novelty stage.[23] British engineer Thomas Savory was the first to make a significant improvement in a steam powered machine when he patented a simple device in 1698 which had no moving parts except for the taps, but could pump water for mining, public use or firefighting.[24] Savory also invented a steam powered system that was supposed to row a boat through the water, but the British Navy rejected it, and it never found favor. In 1712, British inventor Thomas Newcomen invented the atmospheric engine, the first steam engine with a piston, and the first that could be used to power machinery, but was sourced almost

---

[21] Thomas Dublin, *Women at Work: The Transformation of Work and Community in Lowell, Massachusetts, 1826-1860* (New York City: Columbia University Press, 1979), xxv; Harriet H. Robinson, *Loom and Spindle, or Life Among the Early Mill Girls* (New York: Thomas Y. Crowell & Company, 1898), 60.

[22] David S. Landes, *The Unbound Prometheus* (Cambridge, UK: Press Syndicate of the University of Cambridge, 1969), 104.

[23] William Rosen, *The Most Powerful Idea in the World: A Story of Steam, Industry and Invention* (Chicago: University of Chicago Press, 2012), 6.

[24] Thomas Savory, *The Miner's Friend, or an Engine to Raise Water by Fire, Described by Captain Thomas Savery* (London: J. McCormick, 62, Paternoster Row, 1829), 22.

exclusively to pump water.[25] Half a century later, in 1776, James Watt made a new type of stationary steam engine available that was about twice as efficient as the Newcomen engine, making it efficient enough to power factories. The invention of other new machines at the time, especially for textile production, could now be powered by steam instead of horses, humans, wind and water. The Watts Steam Engine was the first invention that could adequately replace and surpass factory water wheels in the United States, meaning mills no longer needed to be located by rivers.[26]

Many inventions such as Eli Whitney's cotton gin were first run primitively by hand or horsepower, which was a great improvement over removing cotton bolls from cotton plants by hand. However, steam made machines like the cotton gin more efficient by many factors. Likewise, newly invented textile mill machines, which already were making fabric production faster than possible by hand, generated material at unheard of speeds.[27]

Steam also helped find a way to get the mass-produced products to consumers in the United States by aiding transportation through engines, greatly accelerating the marketing revolution. Robert Fulton was the first inventor to find commercial success in building a boat propelled by steam, making a legendary 32-hour, 150 mile, trip from New York City to Albany on a steamboat called the *Clermont* in 1807, proving its viability to skeptics who had called his idea Fulton's folly.[28] It was the first commercially successful steamboat, making use of a Boulton and Watt steam engine manufactured by a company partly owned by Watt Steam Engine inventor James Watt.[29] This was a pivotal moment in transportation history, as steamboats overcame many shipping challenges, such as depending on the right winds to carry sailboats to their destinations, and the problem of carrying goods by boat upriver, against the current. Steam power meant transportation by water literally no longer depended on the wind, weather

---

[25] Albert Edward Musson and Eric Robinson, *Science and Technology in the Industrial Revolution* (Milton Park, UK: Taylor & Francis, 1989), 48.

[26] Henry Winram Dickinson, *A Short History of the Steam Engine* (Cambridge, UK: Cambridge University Press, 1939). 87.

[27] Ross Thomson, *Structures of Change in the Mechanical Age: Technological Invention in the United States 1790-1865* (Baltimore, MD: The Johns Hopkins University Press, 2009), 32, 75.

[28] Alice Clary Sutcliffe, *Robert Fulton and the "Clermont"* (New York: The Century Company, 1909), 234.

[29] Erich Roll, *An Early Experiment in Industrial Organisation, being a History of the Firm of Boulton & Watt, 1775-1805* (New York: Longmans, Green and Co., 1930), 14.

or seasonal sea currents. The steamboat provided a vehicle to carry goods made possible by steam powered factories to any water accessible area at virtually any time.[30]

Because of a need to distribute goods, some areas in the western part of the country which were not accessible by water were made so by the building of channels such as the Erie Canal. Canals were much faster than other forms of transportation, as trains were in their infancy and were usually made of cast iron because methods of manufacturing steel had not yet been refined as they would be later in the nineteenth century. Inventor Richard Trevithick had pioneered the steam powered train in England in 1810, but it was unreliable, not powerful and many people rightfully feared it was unsafe, resulting in the machines being relegated to mining operations during the First Industrial Revolution.[31]

The First Industrial Revolution impacted American culture in many ways including a move by younger people to cities to find work in factories. Toward the end of the First Industrial Revolution these large, closely populated cities proved to be a prime market for the product of other innovations, specifically the printing press. At the beginning of the First Industrial Revolution, the printing press remained essentially the same as it had since its invention by Johannes Gutenberg in 1440, comprised mainly of a screw mechanism that squeezed ink onto paper with moveable type. However, several innovations during the First Industrial Revolution quickly changed printing capacity and speed.[32]

In around 1800 Lord Charles Stanhope in England invented a printing press that was a major improvement. Before Stanhope, printing press frames were made of wood. Stanhope made his of solid cast iron, the metal most used at the time for machinery that required strength, as steel processing was so inefficient at the time that its use was mostly confined to cutlery. Stanhope's invention increased the force of the platen on the paper, the effort needed for each pressing, the speed of operation and the printing area. Compared to later advances, this wasn't a great enhancement, as it only increased the

---

[30] Ronald E. Shaw, *Canals for a Nation: The Canal Era in the United States, 1790-1860* (Lexington, KY: University of Kentucky, 2014), Preface.
[31] Dickinson, *A Short History of the Steam Engine*, 97-8.
[32] James Moran, *Printing Presses: History and Development from the Fifteenth Century to Modern Times* (Los Angeles: University of California Press, 1978), 123; William Savage, *A Dictionary of the Art of Printing* (London: Longman, Brown, Green, and Longmans, 1841), 595.

number of papers produced an hour by twenty-five percent, moving from two hundred an hour to two hundred and fifty an hour. However, it stirred interest in printing innovation.[33]

German inventor Koenig began innovating the printing press in 1802. By 1810 he had added cylinders and used steam to power the mechanics. After patenting his invention, Koenig partnered with Andreas Friedrich Bauer to manufacture the presses which he sold to *The Times of London* in 1814. *The Times* used them to create 1,000 to 1,100 pressings an hour, a pace which was about 20 times faster than the Stanhope press. The speed of the Koenig press paved the way for the mass marketing of newspapers and revolutionized book making, although its full capacity as a mass media device had to wait for the right time and a person with the vision to harness its power.[34]

One effect of improved printing methods was increased literacy, which resulted in a demand for more printed material. This, and the movement of people to urban centers where product distribution was cheaper, faster and more profitable resulted in a situation that transformed information dissemination.[35]

Newspapers were well established by the time the First Industrial Revolution came to the United States, although it existed in a very different form and was conceptually evolving on its own. Before the American Revolution, newspapers often had small circulations and some were subsidized by the government and under government control, a time often called the Colonial Press Era. After the American Revolution, political parties took over the subsidization of newspapers and it was during this Partisan Press Era that the First Industrial Revolution began.[36]

One characterizing factor of the early Partisan Press Era was the cost of a single newspaper, six cents a copy, a prohibitive amount for most people but well in reach of the elite. Sales were almost exclusively by subscription, thereby raising the cost even more, because most day laborers could not afford the one-time payment of a subscription. The content was also aimed

---

[33] Ghita Stanhope and George Peabody Gooch, *The Life of Charles, Third Earl of Stanhope* (London: Longmans, Green and Company, 1914), 261.
[34] Philip B. Meggs, *A History of Graphic Design* (Hoboken, NJ: John Wiley & Sons, Inc. 1998), 130.
[35] Kuypers, *Partisan Journalism*, 16.
[36] Carole Sue Humphrey, *The Press of the Young Republic, 1783-1833* (Westport, CT: Greenwood Press, 1996), 41.

at an elite audience, replete with economic interest items and often one-sided political discourse.[37]

While the First Industrial Revolution created a perfect storm of favorability for mass marketing newspapers, it took the ingenuity of Benjamin Day in 1833 to realize its potential. Day began a period often called the Penny Press Era described in more detail in Chapter Two, whereby he sold newspapers to the common people rather than the elite, establishing many of the news story norms that we still have today. It was a change that could only have taken place with the foundation set by the First Industrial Revolution, which created the audience, the means of distribution, the method of printing and the availability of raw materials.[38]

While the First Industrial Revolution is considered to have ended in the 1830s, its influence continued with further innovations and cultural shifts. Among the challenges was the nature of the media, having grown so dominant that it was a force in public opinion. Information was no longer controlled just by the elites and allowed to trickle down to the common people but was delivered cheaply directly to the masses. Although some welcomed this innovation, the fact that the owners of influential newspapers had no limits and could act with virtual impunity, concerned others. While a good printing press owner was seen as someone who could educate the masses positively, it was believed a malicious publisher could just as easily lead society down a negative path. Therefore, it was this belief that the exponentially expanding unregulated media needed ethical journalists at its helm that pushed news workers to create standards of work as a way to define good journalism and to offer guidelines for those who held public sway.[39]

## The Digital Age

The Digital Age, also called the Information Age and the Third Industrial Revolution, began in the 1950s and continues to this day. Initiated at the time when technology began to rely on computer systems, perhaps the Digital Age's greatest impact has been felt in the last two decades, when the

---

[37] David A. Copeland, The *Antebellum Era: Primary Documents on Events from 1820 to 1860* (Westport, CT: Greenwood Publishing Group, 2003), 163.
[38] David R. Spencer, *The Yellow Journalism: The Press and America's Emergence as a World Power* (Evanston, IL: Northwestern University Press, 2007), 22.
[39] Stephen A. Banning, "Unearthing the Origin of Journalistic Professionalization in the Mid-Nineteenth Century" (Master's thesis, University of Missouri, 1993), 13.

World Wide Web and social media in particular transformed the news delivery universe. As evidence of the adaptation of social media in people's lives, social media company owners have become among the wealthiest individuals.[40] So strong is the social media attraction that it has become the main news source for many. According to a Pew Research Center Poll, social media has become the dominant source of news for two-thirds of U.S. adults, meaning a medium which essentially did not exist twenty years ago, now has greater news distribution than traditional news outlets such as newspapers, magazines, radio, network television and cable.[41]

One of the problems that individuals in the Digital Age are facing is the inability of media observers to track where people are getting information, making it difficult to locate the source of disinformation and causing complications such as the Russian interference with the 2016 presidential election. It was not until after the election that it was discovered how much a Russian group had been spreading misinformation on Twitter and Facebook. Some of the information appears to have been published to make individuals lose faith in the election process, but reports suggest some was aimed at undermining presidential candidate Hillary Clinton, who was not considered a supporter of Russia.[42]

## Discussion Questions

1. Remember: What inventions were part of the First Industrial Revolution? Identify as many as you can.

2. Understand: How did the technical changes in the First Industrial Revolution affect culture? Describe life before and after the First Industrial Revolution started.

---

[40] Rob Wile, "Mark Zuckerberg Has Made More Money Than Anyone Else in 2017—Even Jeff Bezos," *Money*, August 8, 2017, http://time.com/money/4891103/mark-zuckerberg-jeff-bezos-billionaires-net-worth-2017/.

[41] "News Use Across Social Media Platforms 2017," *Pew Research Center*, August 23, 2017, http://www.journalism.org/2017/09/07/news-use-across-social-media-platforms-2017/pi_17-08-23_socialmediaupdate_0-01/.

[42] Kathleen Hall Jamison, *Cyber Wars: How Russian Hackers and Trolls Helped Elect a President: What We Don't, Can't, and Do Know* (New York City: Oxford University Press, 2018), 21.

3. Apply: How would we be living today without the technological changes that have occurred since before the First Industrial Revolution?

4. Evaluate: What was the impact of technology during the First Industrial Revolution on newspaper audiences at the time it was occurring?

5. Create: Similar to the mechanical progress that was made during the First Industrial Revolution, we are in a period of technological momentum in modern times. How do you think the technological improvements in the past twenty years have impacted how, where and when we see or hear information?

# CHAPTER TWO

## FINDING PROBLEMS: MASS COMMUNICATION COMES WITH COMPLICATIONS

In Chapter One we discussed how the Penny Press was the child of the Industrial Revolution, which resulted in a change in technology, creating mass media for the first time. In this chapter we look at the ethical problems this caused, as entrepreneurs learned lies could be more profitable than truth. Therefore, this chapter illustrates how technical progress generated new ethical problems in the nineteenth century in the same way that technical progress in modern times has produced ethical problems in the twenty-first century. Later chapters will look at what can be done about it, but this chapter shows how the first years of mass media included a high volume of what would later be considered unethical conduct.

### Affordable News

The Penny Press became possible in the United States because of changes caused by the Industrial Revolution. The steam press invention allowed for the mass production of newspapers, and in the 1830s, publishers created a mass-produced inexpensive newspaper which was sold on the sidewalks. In short, this newspaper revolution used steam presses to mass produce newspapers with new content, at a new price to a new audience in a new place.[1]

The Penny Press newspapers charged one cent for the newspapers, a change from the previous price of six cents, which only the landed gentry could afford. The content was non-political, in order to appeal to an urban working audience, and was sold on street corners, shifting from the previously used subscription service. The previous subscription newspapers had been politically oriented, while the new Penny Press newspapers were politically

---

[1] Philip B. Meggs and Alston W. Purvis, *History of Graphic Design* (Hoboken, NJ: John & Sons, 2016), 158.

neutral and used sensational headlines to assure street sales.[2] The new format was an immense commercial success, becoming the standard for most newspapers in the country.[3]

The first two highly successful Penny Press newspapers were Benjamin Day's *Sun* in 1833 and James Gordon Bennett's *New York Herald* in 1835. Day started out as a reporter in Springfield, Massachusetts, where he learned the value of telling a good story. The idea for a new kind of press originated through a cholera epidemic which spread to the area where Day worked. Because of the widespread illness, the newspaper for which Day worked almost went bankrupt, as there were too few individuals buying newspaper subscriptions to keep it stable and as a result, Day began to think about producing a newspaper that would harness the untapped market of the working class. Consequently, he initiated his own newspaper in New York City called the *Sun*.[4]

Day started small, with a first run of just three-hundred newspapers. He had contracted with a New York City printer on Ann Street, which today is in the heart of the Manhattan business district, just a few blocks from where the 9/11 Memorial stands today. While there were select wealthy individuals in New York City who could afford a subscription to the six-penny newspapers, there were thousands more who could afford a one-penny paper, so Day aimed the newspaper at the city's maids, clerks and factory workers. Ignoring presidential politics and issues like banking that crowded the columns in six-penny party newspapers, Day focused on news from the crime beat such as murders and assaults, as he wanted to give common people something to talk about with others. Success was almost immediate, and in six months, Day was selling roughly double the number of newspapers than the next highest circulating newspaper. He continued to experiment and two years later he published a story about the moon that was false, a fabrication that had been made up from scratch. The fantastic story talked about aliens who roamed the surface of the moon, a fact purportedly discovered by a scientist with a powerful telescope. However outlandish, many newspaper readers believed it. From that, Benjamin Day saw the

---

[2] Sidney Kobre, *Development of American Journalism* (Dubuque, IA: Wm. C. Brown Company Publishers, 1969), 314-15.
[3] James L. Crouthamel, *Bennett's New York Herald and the Rise of the Popular Press* (Syracuse, NY: Syracuse University Press, 1989), 24.
[4] David R. Spencer, *The Yellow Journalism: The Press and America's Emergence as a World Power* (Evanston, IL: Northwestern University Press, 2007), 22.

potential of sensational headlines, regardless of their veracity.[5]

Day's press worked so well, other newspapers duplicated his model, although one imitator stood out more than the others. James Gordon Bennett was an immigrant to the United States who commenced his operation in a sparse basement office located on Wall Street.[6] He shared the same printer that published Day's *Sun*, although Day was not happy about that arrangement, and soon found another printer. Bennett had few resources when he started out, and he is said to have begun with five hundred dollars, a desk made from a piece of wood on two grocery store boxes and a chair. He was also the only employee.[7] Like Day, Bennett used sensationalism to attract readers to an affordable newspaper, leading the *New York Herald* to become the largest in the United States.[8]

## Penny Press Influence Today

Many of the ways we present information today, started with the Penny Press. For example, attention grabbing headlines are still used today in platforms from Facebook and YouTube to Instagram and Twitter. Using headlines was important for the Penny Press newspapers because they invited sidewalk sales, which depended on content that attracted the attention of people on the street, a method much different from the previous system of subscription sales, that was not dependent on sensationalism.[9]

Another Penny Press innovation was the beat system, where specific reporters were assigned to a topic, and at its inception, it meant reporters concentrated in an area such as crime or politics.[10] Today, individuals with access to YouTube can create a channel where he or she talks about an area of expertise, from fashion and DIY (Do-It-Yourself projects) to LPTs (Life Pro Tips). The Penny Press also introduced the idea of interviews to make

---

[5] Willard Grosvenor Bleyer, *Main Currents in the History of American Journalism* (Boston: Houghton Mifflin, 1927), 158-61.

[6] George Henry Payne, *History of Journalism in the United States* (New York: D. Appleton-Century Company, Incorporated, 1940), 261.

[7] Isaac Clarke Pray, *Memoirs of James Gordon Bennet and His Times* (New York: Stringer & Townsend, 1855), 187-8.

[8] Crouthamel, *Bennett's New York Herald,* 37.

[9] Vincent DiGirolamo, *Crying the News: A History of America's Newsboys* (New York: Oxford University Press, 2019), 181, 234, 350, 535.

[10] Eileen N. Gilligan, *Competing for News: Reporter's Use of Competition and Cooperation in the Production of News* (Madison, WI: University of Wisconsin Press, 2004), 49.

a story come alive, a concept still heavily used in traditional and social media.[11]

Soon after the Penny Press came about the public began to perceive problems with the new newspaper model in that the truth was sometimes hard to discern among the sensational and lurid narratives where facts were not allowed to interfere with a good headline that would sell newspapers. Because of this, many individuals felt the Penny Press newspapers appealed to only the lowest human appetites.[12]

## Objectivity

One of the important changes that occurred because of the Penny Press was non-partisan reports. Before the Penny Press Era, all news was generally partisan. In fact, as mentioned briefly in Chapter One, the time period before the Penny Press was called the Party Press Era or Partisan Press Era, when individual publishers were devoted to one political view, depending on partisan subscribers and political patronage for income. The subscribers supported the newspaper's position, and political patronage came from politicians and political parties. Because of this one-sided support, the newspapers were essentially political parties' public relations organizations. At the time, this was better than the situation in the previous Colonial Press Era, where free speech had at times been limited. The Partisan Press Era publishers reveled in the fact that they could criticize the government openly without being punished, something they had not been able to do under British rule without fears of reprisal. The disadvantage was that the Partisan Press was bitterly one-sided and often untruthful. In contrast, the Penny Press publishers avoided one-sidedness, which allowed them to sell newspapers to a wider consumer base, an important factor for newspapers relying on sidewalk sales.[13] Later, the idea of non-partisan reporting became a sign of a professional journalist, as journalists and the public alike forgot that the origin of non-partisan reporting was a system based on making money, not upholding moral standards. After the Civil War, non-partisan reporting became known as independent journalism and was included in the

---

[11] James L. Aucoin, *The Evolution of American Investigative Journalism* (Columbia, MO: University of Missouri Press, 2006), 24.

[12] David B. Sachsman and David W. Bulla, eds., *Sensationalism: Murder, Mayhem, Mudslinging, Scandals, and Disasters in 19ᵗʰ Century Reporting* (Piscataway, NJ: Transaction Publishers, 2013), xxi.

[13] Michael Schudson, *Discovering the News: A Social History of American Newspapers* (New York: Basic Books, 1981), 4.

twentieth century Canons of Journalism. In the twentieth century and today, non-partisan reporting is often called objective reporting or impartiality.[14]

As long as the press has existed, it has influenced how leaders communicated to their constituents or subjects. For instance, the Partisan Press became the way officials communicated to their supporters. There were no presidential press conferences during the days of the Partisan Press, and if the president had something to say, he talked to the publishers who supported him, who printed what he said. The opposition newspapers would then react to what the president had said, and the cycle would continue. When the Penny Press became popular and non-partisan, politicians had to find other ways to be heard, a situation that we still have today in that those in politics find ways to get attention, such as by creating controversy.[15]

## The Penny Press' Ethical Advertising Challenges

The Penny Press introduced a new form of marketing that was the beginning of modern advertising, while also initiating credibility problems for nineteenth century communicators. Advertising had been used in the United States long before the Penny Press Era, as during the Colonial Press Era, newspapers in the United States contained some advertising, although the newspapers were expensive and mostly focused on business, containing information about ships and merchant sales.[16]

The Penny Press advertising had a completely different readership, because for the first-time newspaper advertising was aimed at a mass audience. The first major products advertised in Penny Press newspapers were patent medicines, which sold so well that many newspapers became completely dependent on advertising them. Patent medicines were not new to the United States, existing long before, but there had been no way to mass market them. However, with the advent of the Penny Press, there was a cheap way to reach a mass working class audience, one that might not be able to afford

---

[14] Edwin Ford and Edwin Emery, *Highlights in the History of the American Press: A Book of Readings* (Minneapolis, MN: University of Minnesota Press, 1954), 153; Schudson, *Discovering the News*, 7.

[15] Frank Luther Mott, *American Journalism: A History of Newspapers in the United States Through 250 Years 1690 to 1940* (New York: Macmillan Company, 1945), 113-14.

[16] James Melvin Lee, *History of American Journalism* (New York: Garden City Publishing Co., Inc., 1923), 226.

going to a doctor and would be willing to rely on miracle promising medicines.[17]

Patent medicines in the nineteenth century were substances sold by unlicensed individuals in bottles, tins and pill boxes. The elixirs were said to cure various medical ailments and were usually sold by mail order. At the time, there were no laws about medicines, selling them or using the mail for fraud. Therefore, the medical merchants were not required to list the actual ingredients of a substance sold as medicine, or to have proof that it was ameliorative. The sellers could make any claims in a newspaper advertisement and were not even responsible if the medicine resulted in death. It was not until the beginning of the twentieth century that the government began to regulate medicine, which was the beginning of the end of the patent medicine trade.[18]

## Patent Fraud

Because of a lack of legal requirements, a patent medicine dealer could legally sell flavored water and claim that it cured cancer. Additionally, many patent medicine venders began to use grain alcohol as a base supplemented with addictive drugs such as heroin and cocaine. These were sometimes listed on the label, but usually they were not, as patent medicine sellers did not want anyone to know what was in the concoctions, which they often claimed contained exotic ingredients such as mysterious swamp roots or rare foreign oils. This claim of exclusive ingredients served two purposes. First, it attracted buyers who might otherwise acquire medicine from their neighborhood pharmacist, and, second, it prevented pharmacists from duplicating the product. The patent medicine sellers often claimed exclusive knowledge of the world of medicine and warned users from sampling any other brand prepared by practitioners not privy to their secrets.[19]

---

[17] Erika Janik, *Marketplace of the Marvelous: The Strange Origins of Modern Medicine* (Boston: Beacon Press, 2014), 192.

[18] Paul Starr, *The Social Transformation of American Medicine: The Rise of a Solemn Profession and the Making of a Vast Industry* (New York: Basic Books, 1982), 132.

[19] Arthur Joseph Cramp, *"Patent Medicines" The Nostrum and the Public Health: Truth in Advertising Drug Products* (American Medical Association Bureau of Investigation, Chicago: 1923), 2; W. F. Bynum, *Science and the Practice of*

The secrecy of the substances' content meant that taking too much of it could result in a fatal overdose. Additionally, there was nothing to indicate how much of the substance individuals could take by body weight, and the concentrations varied from bottle to bottle. Additionally, the addictive quality of some of the medicines' ingredients, including alcohol, heroin and morphine, helped assure repeat sales, a situation that continued until the Food and Drug Administration (FDA) was formed in 1906.[20]

One of the difficulties in regulating the patent medicines was the lack of sophistication in medicine at the time. For instance, doctors were still removing patients' blood as a treatment for diseases throughout the nineteenth century and into the twentieth century, a process known as bloodletting, and manufacturers produced specific medical instruments for this common process. Therefore, with limited knowledge and laws not in favor of the prosecution, it was difficult for anyone to prove a patent medicine was fake when it was supposedly made from an exotic secret ancient Native American recipe or the oil from an African tree.[21]

## Profit from Pain

One example of patent medicine financial success involved Benjamin Brandreth, who sold pills containing a strong laxative which Brandreth claimed was imperative for good health.[22] He published books and pamphlets, written in lofty literary prose, pretending to cite scientific information supporting the value of his pills. A Congressional report claimed Brandreth was the most successful patent medicine advertiser of his time, acquiring $600,000 in one year alone, and providing him with the means to become a politician and bank president.[23] In 1858, investigative writer Dan King claimed in the book *Quackery Unmasked*: "These are no mere fancy sketches, but true reports of cases which have often occurred;

---

*Medicine in the Nineteenth Century* (New York: Cambridge University Press, 1996), 165.

[20] Linda Lawson, *Truth in Publishing: Federal Regulation of the Press's Business Practices* (Carbondale, IL: Southern Illinois University Press, 1993), 34.

[21] "Propaganda for Reform," *Journal of the American Medical Association* 67, no. 4 (December 9, 1916): 1774.

[22] Charles E. Rosenberg and William H. Helfand, *"Every Man his Own Doctor" Popular Medicine in Early America* (Philadelphia: Library Company of Philadelphia, 1998), 38.

[23] U. S. *House Journal,* "Patent Medicines," House Report No. 52, 30th Cong., 1849, 31.

and every thoughtful mother should know that all printed recommendations of nostrums are falsehoods, and that every such article is more or less dangerous, is always liable to do more harm than good, and should be shunned."[24] King then proceeded to call out Brandreth by name.[25]

Another famous patent medicine brand was Lydia Pinkham's Vegetable Compound. In the last part of the nineteenth century it was said to be the most popular patent medicine and was a household name. Aimed exclusively at women, it did not contain harmful products such as cocaine or heroin, but did include twenty percent alcohol by volume.[26]

The first patent medicine problem for newspapers came when deaths and addictions occurred, and the newspapers refused to stop carrying the advertisements. The newspapers claimed those attacking the patent medicines were free to take out advertising against them, but that it was not the newspaper's responsibility to investigate its advertising. The newspapers which accepted patent medicine advertising claimed individuals had a right to advertise in the newspaper if payment was made, suggesting that those complaining about the products write to the patent medicine makers rather than the newspaper. Journalism historian James Melvin Lee commented in 1917 that medicine manufacturers "maintain that it is just as honorable to advertise a product which will relieve a stomach of an ache as it is to advertise a mincemeat that puts an ache in the stomach."[27]

The worst offender in advertising patent medicines in New York City was the Penny Press newspaper the *New York Herald*, owned by Penny Press pioneer James Gordon Bennett, who was adamant that he would not refuse any patent medicine advertising for any reason. It was rumored that Bennett had a great financial motive in that he charged patent medicine advertisers twice the normal advertising rate. Eventually, however, Bennett bent to public opinion and limited patent medicine advertising, admitting that patent medicines were the worst kind of advertising. Bennett's turn around in attitude may have been the result of concern that changing attitudes

---

[24] Dan King, *Quackery Unmasked* (New York: D. Clapp, 1858), 294-5.

[25] King, *Quackery Unmasked,* 295.

[26] Sarah Stage, *Female Complaints: Lydia Pinkham and the Business of Women's Medicine* (New York: W. W. Norton and Co., 1979), 53; James Harvey Young, *American Health Quackery: Collected Essays of James Harvey Young* (Princeton, NJ: Princeton University Press, 1992), 5; Stewart Holbrook, *The Golden Age of Quackery* (New York: Collier Books, 1959), 63.

[27] James Melvin Lee, *History of American Journalism* (New York: Houghton Mifflin, 1917), 391.

regarding advertising patent medicines would hurt his circulation.[28] This kind of response undermined the credibility of the newspaper and cast the publishers in the role of robber barons who were unconcerned about society, the opposite of what ethical publishers in the nineteenth century wanted, in trying to be recognized as professionals looking out for society.

It may seem strange that the unlicensed medicines were advertised for so long. However, both the patent medicine sellers and the newspapers reaped great financial rewards, making it a relationship that built many mansions. Additionally, it was unlikely that newspaper or magazine owners who used patent medicine advertising would criticize the product which made them wealthy. Given this, it is ironic that it was a journalism article which finally exposed the dangers of patent medicines in 1905. The FDA was founded a year later partly as a result of this article. The FDA introduced sweeping changes, including a requirement that contents be accurately included on the product label, although it was not until 1938 that certain dangerous substances were banned.[29]

## Fake Healers and Real Journalism

A few articles had been written about the dangers of patent medicines in the nineteenth century, but they were rare. The journalist who made the difference was Samuel Hopkins Adams, writing a series of articles in *Colliers* magazine that were later reprinted by the American Medical Association. Adams studied the companies, wrote articles and named names, listing specific false claims and misrepresentations by the patent medicine companies and explaining how people were being swindled with addictive and sometimes fatal drugs.[30]

He also called out newspapers for being complicit in the fraud. Adams showed how the patent medicine sellers' lies could not be spread without the newspapers' deliberate help, and disclosed that newspapers refused to

---

[28] Bleyer, *Main Currents in the History of American Journalism*, 201-2.
[29] James Harvey Young, *Pure Food: Securing the Federal Food and Drugs Act of 1906* (Princeton, NJ: Princeton University Press, 1914), 216, 276, 289; Arthur Philip Greeley, *The Food and Drugs Act, June 30, 1906* (Washington, DC: John Byrne and Company, 1907), iii-iv. See also: James Harvey Young, *Toadstool Millionaires: A Social History of Patent Medicines in America before Federal Regulation* (Princeton, NJ: Princeton University Press, 1961).
[30] Samuel V. Kennedy, III, *Samuel Hopkins Adams and the Business of Writing* (Syracuse, NY: Syracuse University Press, 1999), 44-5.

print anything negative about patent medicines because of the income they produced. Adams explained: "The retail price of all the patent medicines sold in the United States in one year may be very conservatively placed at one hundred million dollars. And of this one hundred millions [sic] which the people of the United States pay for patent medicines yearly, fully forty millions [sic] goes to the newspapers."[31] Adjusted for inflation, the amount going to newspapers today from patent medicine advertising would be about a billion dollars a year. Adams went on to say that the Lydia Pinkham company alone spent $1.2 million a year on newspaper advertising. This was at a time when most people made about $500 a year. As a result, Adams' muckraking articles had a profound effect on newspapers and the days of unregulated patent medicines were numbered.[32]

Adams' investigative writing on patent medicines not only shined a light on the need for medical regulation, it also spotlighted the newspaper industry's lack of moral guidelines. For instance, Adams admonished: "With a few honorable exceptions the press of the United States is at the beck and call of the patent medicines. Not only do newspapers modify news possibly affecting these interests, but they sometimes become their active agents."[33] This created a climate favorable to professional ethics among the public and journalism ethics supporters in associations, and even many bottom line minded newspaper owners favored the veneer of professional ethics as a way to regain credibility.

## Hidden Influence: Conflict of Interest

The problem of hidden influence affecting newspapers in the nineteenth century similarly influences many journalists today through a factor called a conflict of interest. Advertising is important for communication in modern times, as in most models, it pays for the communicator to operate. However, improper advertising can damage credibility in the Digital Age as much as it did a century ago. For instance, some popular vloggers with tens of millions of subscribers recommend products on their channels. Many times, these products have been given to the bloggers free of charge and sometimes additional payment has been made for the recommendation. Therefore, the bloggers are less likely to give a bad review on a product, knowing that doing so would result in a loss of sponsorships. This creates a situation

---

[31] Samuel Hopkins Adams, *The Great American Fraud* (Chicago: American Medical Association, 1905), 73.
[32] Adams, *The Great American Fraud, 73.*
[33] Adams, *The Great American Fraud, 5.*

where there is great pressure on the vlogger to ignore a product's faults, either consciously or unconsciously. When viewers and subscribers learn of this, reputation may be lost not only for that vlogger, but for online media content in general.

There is certainly nothing wrong with being an advocate, and advocacy alone is not a conflict of interest. A conflict of interest occurs when an individual claims to be a disinterested third party offering an unbiased opinion, when he or she has a hidden agenda. While neither the agenda nor the advocacy is a problem, deceiving people under a pretense of being unbiased is. Additionally, there is nothing wrong with telling people to buy a certain product, but if the reviewer is getting a secret commission for each product sold or has invested in stocks which rise when product sales go up, there is a conflict of interest. The conflict of interest problem can also happen with politics, occurring when people who advocate a political idea or support for a politician pretend to be free from bias.[34]

Many viewers sincerely believe the reviewers they are seeing are objective and not influenced by a gift, and while this is sometimes true, there is no way to distinguish the biased reviews from the non-biased reviews. On their own, some reviewers acknowledge receiving free items, and while this is more honest, it is still a problem because a person is more likely to give a positive review if he or she has been given something for free. This is because individuals usually evaluate an item in relation to how much it costs them. For instance, an individual is more likely to be critical of shoes that cost $200, than shoes that were a gift and cost nothing.

Conflict of interest also affects journalists directly. For over a century now, companies have been giving journalists free gifts, sometimes in the form of an informational trip to an exotic location under the guise of educating them about their organization. These are called junkets and are usually considered a conflict of interest. For example, in the past, when the author of this book was a journalist, some amusement parks would offer journalists free tickets to their properties twice a year for up to ten people, proposed under the guise of education about their organization, but in reality, it comprised a gift which amounted to a conflict of interest.

Because of conflict of interest concerns, some news organizations have had rules against gifts, mandating that journalists in their employ could not

---

[34] Karin Wahl-Jogensen and Thomas Hanitzsch, *The Handbook of Journalism Studies* (Philadelphia, PA: Routledge, 2009), 372.

accept a gift at all, or were limited to gifts worth under $25. The $25 limit allowed companies to give a token gift to a journalist, such as a bottle of alcohol or an inexpensive lunch, without assuming it would affect reporting. Avoiding conflicts of interest is part of one of the Canons of Journalism to be examined later.

## Yellow Journalism

The Penny Press introduced sensationalism, which occurs when an individual relates a story in a manner that makes it seem more important than it is. There are many reasons to do this, but often the reason is financial in nature. As described earlier in the discussion of the Penny Press, sensationalism came into its own in the nineteenth century when editors discovered sidewalk sales shot up when newspapers had sensational headlines, resulting in news workers shouting the headlines to the public on the street. Editors and publishers quickly realized that lurid and sensational stories sold faster and made more money than those stories which did not have an interesting angle. For instance, stories about rape, murder, divorce or infidelity were sure sellers, and as a result, reporters who could find these stories were rewarded with continued employment, and those who could not, might be fired.[35]

The fact that sensational stories resulted in rewards for both the reporter and the publisher meant there was great pressure to find a continual source of dramatic news, which pressed strapped reporters to bend facts to fashion a more interesting account. At times, entire stories were made up, because fabrication could be more profitable than truth. This situation grew to its worst point from 1895 to 1898 in the Yellow Journalism Era.[36]

Two newspaper entrepreneurs were typical of Yellow Journalism. Newspaper owners William Randolph Hearst and Joseph Pulitzer were fierce rivals, each trying to outdo the other with sensational headlines. Yellow Journalism made Hearst and Pulitzer wealthy as evidenced by Hearst's sprawling castle built in San Simeon, California, on his 250,000-acre property, a tourist attraction to this day. Pulitzer and Hearst defined the Yellow Journalism Era so much that the story of their lives is largely the story of this time period. Relevancy is apparent in that the manner in which they produced their newspapers is analogous to some modern news outlets notorious for their

---

[35] Crouthamel, *Bennett's New York Herald,* 23.
[36] Edwin Emery and Michael Emery, *The Press and America* (Upper Saddle River, NJ: Prentice Hall, 1984), 194.

click-bait headlines.[37]

No one is sure where the term Yellow Journalism came from. However, one theory is that it came from a cartoon called The Yellow Kid. Strangely, both Hearst and Pulitzer had employed Yellow Kid cartoonist Richard Outcault at some time. Pulitzer was the first to have Outcault, a clever artist with a talent for innovation, who was the first to use color cartoons, but after Hearst moved to New York, he hired Outcault away from Pulitzer to work at his own newspaper.[38]

## Pulitzer: Immigrant Millionaire

Pulitzer and Hearst were character opposites. Pulitzer was a scrappy German immigrant who could not speak English when he arrived in the United States. He fought for the Union Army during the Civil War, before going to work in St. Louis, Missouri, at German and later English language newspapers. He quickly rose through the ranks at St. Louis newspapers, especially at one that survives today as the *St. Louis Post-Dispatch*. While there he supervised an important young editor named John Cockerill, who would continue to work with him and play an important part in his organizations.[39]

Pulitzer had not been raised in wealth and had earned everything he had. Part of the reason for his success was that he drove his employees hard and strove tirelessly to be sell more newspapers than his rivals.[40] He was not sophisticated, polite or smooth, or even known as a great journalist, and often his personality grated against those who worked for him. However, few newspapers wanted to compete with him because of his ruthless drive to succeed. Still, moving to New York was a huge gamble, as it was the biggest newspaper market in the world, and it had the heaviest newspaper competition. However, Pulitzer's management of the *New York World* went well, and with his former employee from St. Louis, John Cockerill, running

---

[37] David Elliot Berman, "Breaking Babel: A Comparative Historical Analysis of Yellow Journalism and Clickbait," (paper presented at the AEJMC 2018 annual conference, Washington, DC, 6-9 Aug. 2018).
[38] Joseph W. Campbell, *Yellow Journalism: Puncturing the Myths, Defining the Legacies* (Westport, CT: Praeger Press, 2001), 29; Sidney Kobre, *The Yellow Press and Gilded Age Journalism.* Gainesville, FL: Florida State University, 1964.
[39] Payne, *History of Journalism in the United States,* 363.
[40] W. A. Swanberg, *Pulitzer* (New York: Charles Scribner's Sons, 1967), 75.

day to day operations it soon became a force with which to reckon.[41]

## Hearst's Empire

In stark contrast to Pulitzer, Hearst was rich when he became a publisher and there had not been a time in his life when he had not been wealthy, being born into it with a politically powerful father who owned large timber tracks and mining operations. The elder Hearst became a U.S. Senator and his wife was the first female regent of the University of California, Berkeley. The young Hearst was not like his father. While the younger Hearst initially attended Harvard University, he was expelled for pranks.[42]

Seeing his son idle after leaving Harvard, William Randolph Hearst's father gave him the *San Francisco Examiner* newspaper as a gift, which legend has it, that the elder Hearst was said to have won in a poker game.[43] The younger Hearst did much better in the real world than in school and excelled at the *Examiner*, for while Hearst himself was not a great journalist, he shined at spotting talent and hiring excellent workers.[44]

Early on, Hearst saw himself as becoming a press baron, and to achieve that status, like the Penny Press founders over a century prior, he knew he needed to be successful in the greatest newspaper market in the world, New York City. To make the jump, in 1895, he bought a newspaper, the *New York Morning Journal,* that was in financial straits. The first obstacle that he encountered was the newspapers' lack of talented journalists, and to remedy this, he went where the most talent was, Pulitzer's newspaper. Hearst began a practice he would continue for much of this life, which was to raid talent from other newspapers, often Pulitzer's. This helped his newspaper in three ways. It brought in established journalists, it brought in new readers and it left a hole in his rival's staff. For instance, in taking well known cartoonist Richard Outcault and his Yellow Kid comic from Pulitzer, Hearst was inviting Outcault's fans to try out Hearst's newspaper. In order to entice reporters to work for him, Hearst offered employees of other newspapers more money than they were making under Pulitzer, and because

---

[41] Swanberg, *Pulitzer,* 76.

[42] Brian Denis, *Pulitzer: A Life* (Hoboken, NJ: A Life John Wiley & Sons, Inc., 2001), 196.

[43] Marvin Olasky, *Central Ideas in the Development of American Journalism: A Narrative History* (New York: Routledge, 2016), 112.

[44] Ben Procter, *William Randolph Hearst: The Early Years, 1893-1910* (New York: Oxford University Press, 1998), 81.

there was little loyalty in the New York City world of journalism, reporters were quick to change sides to improve their situations.[45]

Pictures of Hearst suggest a harsh person, but in reality, while he was ruthless with competitors, he could be very good with employees of all kinds. Despite his wealth, he got along well with even the most bohemian of reporters. Because of this, he developed a reputation as a reasonable person to work for, which facilitated his raiding of talent from the *New York World*, as some reporters did not like working with Pulitzer's prickly personality.[46]

Hearst seemed to enjoy the newspaper rivalry and view it as a game, assuming if he failed as a newspaper owner, he still had his father's extensive riches on which to fall back. Pulitzer, however, had been raised in relative poverty and saw the need to save wherever possible. Thus, Pulitzer never matched Hearst's free spending ways, and he never regarded New York journalism's cut-throat competition as sport.[47]

The world had never seen anyone like William Randolph Hearst. At the height of his success, his newspaper chain had more than twenty newspapers. He concentrated ownership of the media in a way that the media had never experienced, and used it to exert influence, demonstrating the civic dangers and financial rewards of such an arrangement.[48]

One of the main historical events during the time of the Yellow Journalism Era was the Spanish-American War, which came at a time when Cuba and the Philippines were Spain's colonies. There was tension between the United States and Spain, but Hearst fanned it into a major concern, doing so much to encourage a war that Hearst is considered one of its causes. To create sensational headlines, Hearst played to the hearts of his readers, describing the torment of Cuban colonialists under Spanish rule and the strip search of a female United States' tourist.[49]

---

[45] George H. Douglas, *The Golden Age of Newspapers* (Westport, CT: Greenwood Press, 1934), 151.

[46] David Nasaw, *The Chief: The Life of William Randolph Hearst* (New York: Houghton Mifflin Company, 2001), 110.

[47] Proctor, *William Randolph Hearst: The Early Years, 1863-1910,* 103.

[48] James McGrath Morris, "William Randolph Hearst," in *Encyclopedia of American Journalism*, Stephen L. Vaughn, ed. (New York: Routledge, 2008), 212.

[49] Alfred McClung Lee, *The Daily Newspaper in America,* (New York: Macmillan Company, 1937), 273, 283. See also: Stephen A. Banning, "John McCutcheon's

The business success of both Pulitzer and Hearst came with a price. In order to produce a constant torrent of sensational headlines, truth was readily sacrificed. Sometimes it was just a headline that simply oversold the story, but in other instances the accounts were demonstrably false, part of a battle of headlines as each newspaper tried to conquer their rivals through sensationalism. In terms of journalism, it brought out the worst of all involved. In some cases, editors did not know that stories were outright false or twisted by the reporter to give it a better angle. However, the main value at the time was having reporters who provided stories that sold newspapers, so truth was of secondary value. In some cases, the Yellow Journalists performed well and acted bravely in wartime situations, but for the most part Yellow Journalism tainted the entire field of reporting.[50]

While fake stories were one consequence of sensationalism, another was that sensational stories often did not help society. When there was not an election or a war to promote, murder, rape and gossip were the headlines bellowed by children hawking newspapers on city sidewalks. Unfortunately, the news items that have a great impact on society like government actions are usually not sensational. For instance, the announcement of a new law that a committee has been working on for months does not have the draw of a gas tanker exploding on a highway, even though many more people may be ultimately be affected by the former. Because of this tendency, a lack of government reporting was one of the reasons journalists in the nineteenth century began to see a problem with sensational reporting as it was not providing an informed electorate.[51]

## Destroying Truth for Profit

Some believe Hearst won the rivalry against Pulitzer, but in terms of ethics, it was a race to the bottom, as both sides made money by publishing reports that could not be trusted. However, it came with a cost to their reputations. Regarding Hearst, author Louis Pizzitola described the situation aptly in noting: "It is an indication of Hearst's reputation in the United States that so many people were ready to believe the worst in him."[52]

---

Asian Adventure: A Nineteenth-Century Adventure Journalist Covers the Battle for Manila Bay from the Inside," *Journalism History* 42, no. 1 (Spring 2016): 31-40.
[50] Campbell, *Yellow Journalism,* 119.
[51] Emery and Emery, *The Press and America*, 239.
[52] Louis Pizzitola, *Hearst Over Hollywood: Power, Passion, and Propaganda in the Movies* (New York: Columbia University Press, 2002), 222.

One of the things that damaged Hearst's reputation and the Yellow Press in general, was reporting related to a presidential assassination. In 1901, United States President William McKinley was assassinated by a man named Leon Czolgosz. However, before the assassination, Hearst papers had run stories which portrayed McKinley as an evil man, criticizing him harshly. Therefore, after the assassination, the public turned on Hearst, blaming him for McKinley's death. Thus, Hearst's strength in having newspapers that stirred public controversy also contributed to his downfall.[53]

Hearst's newspapers stated it was a champion for the people and claimed to be able to influence people to act. The *New York Journal's* slogan was "While others talk, the Journal acts." This assertion had some truth, as the newspaper chain was influential. Therefore, when the Hearst newspaper chain viciously attacked McKinley who was then killed by an anarchist, the public held Hearst responsible. At the time, anarchists were anti-government individuals who used violent means to gain visibility, the Chicago Haymarket Square bombing being one example of anarchist action. After the McKinley assassination, Hearst continued to run his newspaper chain, but the costs of the public's assassination accusations caught up him and he ran into financial trouble.[54]

While Yellow Journalism made millions, some individuals found the actions of Hearst and Pulitzer repulsive including one editor, Adolf Ochs, from Chattanooga, Tennessee, who had an opportunity to buy a failing newspaper in New York City in 1896. Ochs purchased the *New York Times* at a time when Yellow Journalism was tarnishing the image of the newspaper business. He wanted his newspaper to be a contrast to Yellow Journalism, and so he adopted the slogan "All the news that's fit to print," which is still on the *New York Times* masthead today.[55] Ochs advertised the new journalistic direction by saying of his newspaper, "It does not soil the breakfast cloth."[56] By this Ochs meant it did not contain sex and graphic crime merely as a ploy to draw in readers, because he believed that the public was tired of Yellow Journalism, and that a serious, credible, newspaper could do well. He was correct and the paper turned around quickly.[57]

---

[53] Proctor, *William Randolph Hearst,* 115.

[54] Nasaw, *The Chief: The Life of William Randolph Hearst,* 156-7.

[55] Schudson, *Discovering the News*, 112.

[56] Elmer Holmes Davis, *History of the New York Times, 1851-1921* (New York: Press of J.J. Little & Ives, Co., 1921), 224.

[57] Emery and Emery, *The Press and America*, 238.

# Drama Triumphs Over Truth

Sensationalism is a problem which is just as prominent in digital media, where story titles may be used to entice web surfers to click a link to a particular story. Because online advertising is usually measured with click-through rates, the headline is vital for the business model to be financially successful. A headline that is not eye catching is unlikely to get high click-through rates, and consequently, a sensational headline has a higher likelihood of financial renumeration. Therefore, sensational headlines make more money. In the end, advertisers and content providers in the Digital Age survive based on successful click-through rates.[58]

The result of sensationalism both now and in the past is that individuals become skeptical of all news. For instance, when a high percentage of headlines leave members of the public feeling that they had been misled, they tend to stop clicking as often. This in turn, leads to a vicious cycle, because to entice skeptical web surfers to click on links, content providers must make the headlines more outrageous. Thus, the ultimate casualty of sensationalism is truth, because there is not enough sensational information in the world to satisfy content providers' needs. For instance, the eruption of a major volcano with ash that may disrupt international air travel is both true and sensational. However, this kind of event does not happen frequently enough to satisfy a need for sensational headlines, and eventually relatively unimportant reports are exaggerated to meet the voracious demand for titillating headlines, often leaving unreported the information needed to provide for an informed electorate.[59]

# Newspapers Turn to Professionalism to Restore Credibility

The move to professionalize journalism in the early twentieth century had been a long time in coming. It was the culmination of attempts to curb newspaper excesses that had begun in the Penny Press Era. It was also a way to make changes that had been caused by technology acceptable to society.

---

[58] Marc-David L. Seidel, "Factors Impacting Click-Through Rate," in *Encyclopedia of Social Media and Politics*, Kerrick Harvey, ed. (Thousand Oaks, CA: Sage Publications, 2014), 281.
[59] Victor Pickard, *Democracy without Journalism? Confronting the Misinformation Society* (New York: Oxford University Press, 2019), 79.

Newspapers did not move toward supporting self-imposed regulations by themselves, and it is an important point that newspapers first issued widely used codes of ethics at a time when other industries faced government regulation. Newspapers chose to self-regulate at a time when the federal government was stepping in to regulate many industries such as drugs, banking, transportation, insurance and interstate selling. Some historians call this time period the Progressive Era, because it was an interval when society finally began to draw up rules to protect itself from changes initiated by the First Industrial Revolution. In the next chapter we will look at how some journalists tried to create a standard for the newspaper system that the First Industrial Revolution had helped create, a system of professionalization used in hopes it would generate confidence in newspapers undermined by sensationalism.

## Discussion Questions

1. Remember: What are the meanings of the terms "bias," "partisan information" and "sensationalism?"

2. Understand: What are the moral implications of each of the above terms and how they could affect a news site, the reputation of a company and the ability to advertise on a site?

3. Apply: Use the internet to find three stories, one each, exemplifying bias, partisan information and sensationalism. Can you explain the writer's reasoning behind each, and identify at least three motivations?

4. Evaluate: How would you justify a requirement that all information sites purporting to disseminate news be required to display a badge in the upper right-hand corner showing a rating of how credible past stories have been?

5. Create: How would you describe and defend what changes you would make to solve the problems created by bias, partisan information and sensationalism?

# CHAPTER THREE

# WORKING TOWARD A SOLUTION: ATTEMPTS AT PROFESSIONALIZATION

Even though some publishers found wealth, helming powerful newspapers from the start of the mass media and beyond, many were aghast at the state of journalism. While the last chapter examined the creation of mass media, this chapter reveals how journalists reacted to what they saw as a dereliction of duty by the press barons such as Bennett and Day, which led to discussions of professionalization and journalism standards of work. These journalism standards of work lay the foundation for two codes of ethics that would achieve widespread acceptance early in the twentieth century.[1]

The First Industrial Revolution ended around the 1840s, but societal changes were still in their nascent stage. For instance, the First Industrial Revolution introduced the phenomenon of modern factories, which required many workers, so the factories were usually in cities, attracting many from rural areas. Consequently, this increased the size of cities, creating a population ripe for mass marketing. The mass markets then created a consumer class eager to buy the goods created by the factories. This metamorphosis from an agrarian to a market culture transformed commerce, as people began to rely less on themselves for basic needs, and more on society.[2]

The professionalism movement in the 1800s was seen as a way to organize the newly formed complex society in order to provide accountability for powerful individuals who had the potential to do a great deal of harm or good to society. Society generally embraced the professionalization movement as it guaranteed a level of expertise that they believed was needed to guide

---

[1] Hazel Dicken-Garcia, *Journalistic Standards in Nineteenth Century America* (Madison, WI: University of Wisconsin Press, 1989), 240.
[2] Peter N. Stearns, *The Industrial Revolution in World History* (Boulder, CO: Westview Press, 1998), 61.

the newly transformed civilization.[3] Therefore, this chapter appraises the journalism professionalization movement that occurred in the second half of the nineteenth century which acquired the hallmarks of professionalization: professional organizations, university education and widely used codes of ethics.

## Society Reinvents Itself

In the nineteenth century professionalization would help society find some equilibrium. Emile Durkheim, one of the first sociologists, wrote about the culture around him toward the end of the nineteenth century, trying to comprehend how society functioned. He came up with an explanation called Functionalism, which posited that there are distinctive elements of society, and when one fluctuates, the others follow suit.[4] Durkheim observed this phenomenon during the First Industrial Revolution and in the changes that continued to transpire years later, illustrating that the larger social structure was responsive to elemental deviations. Durkheim's Functionalism helps us understand how technological advances have affected existing society as well. Durkheim said a society that was well adjusted to exogenous forces was in equilibrium. Because the changes in our current Digital Age are great, it may take time for society to reach this stage. Additionally, the fact that technology continues to develop, means equilibrium may take even longer to achieve.[5]

## A Call for Experts

The way professionalism affected the United States is important in understanding journalism ethics because it was inextricably tied to the formation of journalism standards of work in the mid-nineteenth century. Transformations produced by the Industrial Revolution made individuals feel unsure, and in trying to assuage the insecurity, they turned to professionalization. At the start of the nineteenth century, there were only

---

[3] Magali Sarfatti Larson, *The Rise of Professionalism: A Sociological Analysis* (Berkeley, CA: University of California Press, 1977), 5.
[4] Mark Abrahamson, *Functionalism* (Upper Saddle River, NJ: Prentice-Hall, 1978), 22.
[5] Emile Durkheim, *The Division of Labor in Society* (London: The MacMillan Co., 1933), 182, 368-369.

three professions, although over the course of the nineteenth century many other occupations claimed to be professional as well.[6]

In the 1800s society viewed professions as extremely important, much more so than is currently the case. You can see this in an 1857 book called *The Choice of a Profession* in which the author explained: "The importance of the professions and the professional classes can hardly be overrated. They form the head of the middle class, and maintain its tone and independence, keep up to the mark its standard of morality, and direct its intelligence."[7]

The three classic professions were doctors, lawyers and the clergy, occupations that had evolved over many centuries to have a set of qualifications. It was believed that these vocations were too important and easily abused to be performed by just anyone. Therefore, they required specialized education. The clergy was the first to establish this requirement, with educational institutions going back nine-hundred years, and requiring licensing before a member was allowed to work.[8]

Lawyers also had requirements for training, which varied, including a system of licensing called the Bar. It was not until 1729 in England that lawyers were required to pass an exam on legal matters and then hold a five-year apprenticeship. The licensing exam did not start until 1836 in England. Soon after, lawyers began learning their profession by attending schools called inns, which started in 1854.[9]

Doctors were late to the professionalization game. For most of their early history, they did not have the respect they enjoy today. For instance, in the beginning of the 1700s, many barbers were also surgeons.[10] The two occupations were linked, perhaps because they both required sharp instruments at a time when fine cutting knives were expensive and difficult to sharpen. The barber pole is actually a nod to the days when the local

---

[6] Larson, *The Rise of Professionalism*, 6.

[7] Byerly H. Thomson, *The Choice of a Profession* (London: n. p., 1857), 5.

[8] Howard M. Vollmer and Donald L. Mills, *Professionalization* (Englewood Cliffs, NJ: Prentice-Hall Inc., 1966), 2; Robert Gordon Latham, *Samuel Johnson's A Dictionary of the English Language* (London: Longmans, Green, & Co., 1876), 624.

[9] W. J. Reader, *Professional Men* (London: Weidenfeld and Nicholson, 1966), 21, 27; A.M. Carr-Saunders and P.A. Wilson, *The Professions,* 2nd ed. (London: Frank Cass & Co. Ltd., 1964), 34.

[10] Sven Med Tidskr, "From Barber to Surgeon: The Process of Professionalization," *Svensk Medicinhistorisk Tidskrift* 11, no. 1(2007): 69.

barber could remove the hair from your head or the bullets in your side.[11] Eventually, the medical profession began to require university education and licensing, and laws were established that forbade barbers from performing surgery.[12]

While medical practitioners did not professionalize until the nineteenth century, the realization of the importance of medical education started earlier. The English began to discuss medical education in the 1300s. Even in medieval times, medical degrees were available, although they were not as prestigious as other degrees. However, it took until the end of the 1500s for medical degrees to become a requirement for those who wanted to practice medicine. Despite these early advances, it was not until 1847 that the American Medical Association was formed in the United States.[13]

One way in which doctors learned about the human body in the early days was by examining and dissecting corpses, an important step in their training even though doing so was highly illegal. Despite the fact that they could be punished for buying corpses, they persisted. Because of this underground market in dead bodies, unscrupulous rogues began to rob graves of recently deceased people. One famous pair of men who trafficked in dead bodies in London became serial killers in order to provide medical practitioners with bodies. They were subsequently caught and executed when a doctor recognized a corpse as an individual with whom he had spent time earlier in the week. The fact that doctors were associated with grave robbing had a profound effect on their status. It was soon after that doctors attempted to salvage their reputation through a professionalization process, and by the nineteenth century they were considered one of the three classic professions.[14]

## The Professional Era Arrives

By the end of the Industrial Revolution in the 1830s, the three classic professions had established their bona fides as university education, licensing, codes of ethics and professional associations. Because this occurred while individuals were trying to understand the changes that had happened as a result of the Industrial Revolution, the three classic

---

[11] John Timbs, *Doctors and Patients* (London: R. Bentley and Son, 1873), 226.
[12] William Kitay, *The Challenge of Medicine* (New York: Holt, Rinehart and Winston, 1963), 24.
[13] Daniel Calhoun, *Professional Lives in America* (Cambridge: Harvard University Press, 1965), 20.
[14] Larson, *The Rise of Professionalism*, 4.

professions were seen as the first members of an expert class needed for the new age.[15]

The idea of becoming a professional was attractive to working individuals, as there were great advantages to being considered a professional over a trade worker. The greatest benefit may have been prestige, as it elevated the member to a higher class, although higher pay often followed.[16]

Some scholars question whether journalism was ever a profession, and this depends on the definition of a profession. If the definition demands a license, journalism has never been a profession, because requiring a license would contradict the freedom of speech concept, as freedom of speech requires that all be allowed have a voice, rather than merely those who have acquired licenses.[17] Not all, however, believe that every profession requires a license. Additionally, many leading sociologists who have studied professions consider professionalization a gradual process. Sociologists A. M. Carr-Saunders and P. A. Wilson believed professions gradually grew into higher status through a process that was not smooth. As examples, they cited problems lawyers and doctors encountered in achieving professional status. Sociologist Everett Cherrington Hughes also regarded the process as a gradual procession, viewing professionalization as a series of steps. Likewise, sociologist Wilbert Moore believed that professionalization developed in stages, conceiving that a profession would start out as an occupation, move on to be a calling, get an association, then require education and have more autonomy.[18] Observing it in this manner, there is little doubt that journalism at one time was in the process of professionalization, as written records confirm journalists self-identified as professionals as early as 1853, seventy years before the American Society

---

[15] Philip Elliott, *The Sociology of the Professions* (New York: Herder and Herder, 1973), 40. See also: Robert Dingwall and Philip Lewis, *The Sociology the Professions: Lawyers, Doctors and Others* (New York: St. Martin's Press, 1983).

[16] Stephen A. Banning, "The Professionalization of Journalism: A Nineteenth-Century Beginning," *Journalism History* 24, no. 4 (Winter 1998-1999): 157-60.

[17] John C. Merrill, "Journalistic Professionalization: Danger to Freedom and Pluralism," *Journal of Mass Media Ethics* 1, no. 2 (Spring/Summer 1986): 56.

[18] Carr-Saunders and Wilson, *The Professions*, 3; Everett Cherrington Hughes, *Men and Their Work* (Glencoe, IL: The Free Press, 1958), 134; Wilbert E. Moore, *The Professions: Roles and Rules* (New York: Russell Sage Foundation, 1970), 6, 15-22.

of Newspaper Editors' code of ethics.[19]

## Journalists Consider Professionalism

The professional class was only intended to include those occupations which were vital to society, and because of this, some journalists postulated arguments which framed journalism as the educator of the people and the vehicle of progress. They reasoned that if journalism was entrusted with such a great responsibility, journalists deserved to be part of the professional class, arguing that professionals alone should be delegated to the inordinately influential power of newspapers.[20]

The discussion came from organizations which formed after the Civil War. These state publisher's bodies began forming all over the United States. Most of the groups called themselves professional associations and clearly identified as being professionals, comparing themselves to doctors, lawyers and the clergy. Some also called for university education and codes of ethics.[21]

To many journalists, bad behavior during the Civil War was a perfect example of why society needed a proficient class of trained individuals with university education and a code of ethics, specifically using poor examples of Civil War journalism as an argument for journalism professionalization. Just as doctors had used professionalization to help their reputation which had been damaged by grave robbing, journalists saw professionalization as a way to raise their status as well.[22]

## Civil War and Uncivil Journalism

Journalists in the Civil War had acted badly, with reports of battles and skirmishes rarely covered by embedded reporters like they are today. In fact, the newspaper battle reports were often covered by correspondents who never saw the action and were twenty to thirty miles away from where it had happened. Therefore, coverage was usually based on reports from

---

[19] Stephen A. Banning, "The Maine Press Association Takes a Stand: Promoting Professional Identity in the Nineteenth Century," *Maine Historical Journal*, Forthcoming.
[20] Banning "The Professionalization of Journalism," 157.
[21] Banning "The Professionalization of Journalism," 157.
[22] Philip Knightly, *The First Casualty* (New York: Harcourt, Brace, Jovanovich, 1975), 21-2.

people who might not even have seen the fighting first-hand. As a result, the reporters often got the story wrong, even in situations where reporters were trying to get the truth, and unscrupulous reporters at the time simply made things up. Because there was no way to fact-check the story right away, the reporters' fabrications usually went undiscovered. At the time, many newspapers also paid by the word, which resulted in longer stories regardless of the amount of information a reporter had.[23]

There were a few good reporters during the Civil War like Franc Bangs Wilkie who accurately reported military movements and battles. Wilkie was a college educated newspaper editor who had not been successful in making a living at his occupation until he became a correspondent. Unfortunately, Wilkie stands out because he was so unusual. He told the truth, even when it was not good, and he risked his life to get first-hand accounts of the battles.[24]

Unlike Wilkie, most Civil War reporters were considered crude and low class, described by journalism historian Sidney Kobre as "bohemian in nature."[25] At the time bohemians included writers, actors and visual artists who were often construed as loose living drunkards, understood to be talented, but not fit for polite society. The reporter bohemians were often seen as good storytellers but not as individuals who let the facts interfere with a good narrative.[26]

## Beginnings of Journalism Education

The Civil War occurred about twenty-five years after the Penny Press Era had started, and as a result, society was still becoming acclimated to mass produced newspapers, and reporters were still becoming familiar with their role as societal conduits of information. Because society had not imposed publishing parameters, reporters pushed the envelope in regard to what they thought the public would tolerate. Government officials were sometimes alarmed by newspaper content, and editors who did not support the partisan objectives were sometimes threatened and shut down. Even President

---

[23] Knightly, *The First Casualty*, 21-2.

[24] See Franc Bangs Wilkie, *Personal Reminiscences of Thirty-five Years of Journalism* (Chicago: F. J. Schulte & Company, 1891).

[25] Sidney Kobre, *The Development of American Journalism* (Dubuque, IA: William C. Brown Company Printers, 1969), 732.

[26] James M. Perry, *A Bohemian Brigade, the Civil War Correspondents: Mostly Rough—Sometimes Ready* (Hoboken, NJ: Wiley, 2000), 70, 71.

Lincoln, a former publisher himself, allowed censorship to occur through his military field officers, who had little patience with constitutional details when they were immersed in war.[27]

Philip Knightly' seminal  wartime journalism book *The First Casualty* claims the first casualty in war is truth, and during the Civil War, generals on both sides of the conflict had discovered this. For instance, Union General Ulysses S. Grant had hated reporters from the start for sometimes unfounded negative accounts about him.[28] On the other side, Confederate General Robert E. Lee also disliked war coverage, and took action. After the war ended, Lee started the first university classes in journalism at an institution then called Washington College, now known as Washington and Lee University. However, the program did not last long.[29]

The challenge with the push toward professionalization after the Civil War was that not everyone was on board, and there were a few who even believed university education undermined the concept of a practical printer. Some of the journalists who believed this were the old guard who had risen through the ranks with little formal education. These self-made individuals called themselves practical printers, advocating for experience over higher education, preferring an apprenticeship to several years at a university.[30] One author of a handbook for practical printers in 1884 warned printers against new methods of learning, noting: "In the present day, there is, perhaps, a tendency to rely too heavily on text-books [original spelling]…"[31] Some journalists in metropolitan areas did not support the drive for professionalism either, as the major newspaper owners in cities were mostly focused on financial gain, and the details of how it happened were not a

---

[27] Stephen A. Banning, "'Determined to Suppress Everything Like Free Speech': Lincoln's Private Letters Reveal Aggressive Use of Newspaper Censorship," *Journalism History* 45, no. 1 (Spring 2020): 1-18.

[28] Harry James Maihafer, *The General and the Journalists: Ulysses S. Grant, Horace Greeley and Charles Dana* (McLean, VA: Brassey's Inc., 1998), 35.

[29] William David Sloan, *Makers of the Media Mind: Journalism Educators and Their Ideas* (New York: Routledge, 2014), 3.

[30] Frederic Hudson, *Journalism in the United States from 1690 to 1872* (New York: Harper and Brothers Publishers, 1873), 714; Frank Luther Mott, *American Journalism: A History of Newspapers in the United States Through 250 Years 1690-1940* (New York: Macmillan Company, 1945), 406.

[31] John Southward, *Practical Printing: A Handbook of the Art of Typography* (London: J. M. Powell & Son, 1884), xiv.

concern to them, explaining how Yellow Journalism occurred at a time when some journalists were working to professionalize.[32]

In the twentieth century, a number of communication scholars saw the professional class as detrimental to society. For Marxists, the professional class translated into a cohort called the bourgeoisie, or ruling class, and in the Marxist model, the ruling class unfairly exploits the working class. Therefore, the Marxist view was that the professional model as practiced in the nineteenth century was harmful to society.[33]

## Bohemian Communicators

The metropolitan journalists in the nineteenth century tended to be less professional minded than others, as their fortunes were more likely to be founded on writing sensational stories, a practice frowned on by professionally minded publishers. Cities also had their own media organizations which were different from the state press associations that advocated professionalization. The metropolitan press organizations were called press clubs rather than press associations. The press clubs generally had a specific space near the newspaper offices, and many were little more than drinking clubs. The reporters at the time, mostly single individuals in their early twenties, stopped by daily to tell stories, drink and sleep between shifts. The most notorious of these clubs was Chicago's Whitechapel Club, where members drank whiskey out of human skulls that had been made into drinking cups, while sitting around a coffin that served as their table. The walls were decorated with gruesome evidence from famous murders including a noose that had lynched someone and a piece of the bomb used in the Haymarket Square anarchist incident. Additionally, some of the relics which hung on the walls were covered with dried blood. These were not the trappings of those who claimed a professional identity.[34]

---

[32] Alfred McClung Lee, *The Daily Newspaper in America* (New York: The Macmillan Company, 1937), 659.

[33] See Arthur J. Kaul, "The Proletarian Journalist: A Critique of Professionalization," *Journal of Mass Media Ethics* 1, no. 2 (Spring/Summer 1986): 47; Stephen A. Banning, "Unearthing the Origin of Journalistic Professionalization in the Mid-Nineteenth Century" (Master's thesis, University of Missouri, 1993), 46, 47.

[34] Stephen A. Banning, "Not Quite Professional: Bohemian and Elitist Newspaper Clubs in Nineteenth Century Chicago," *Journalism History* 40, no. 1 (Spring 2014): 2-28.

Many city press clubs in the late nineteenth century were an example of the bohemian press clubs that had sprung up at the time in New York City and San Francisco. Like the bohemian writers in the Civil War, the bohemian clubs were anti-establishment conclaves for artists of all kinds and usually closed after a few years because they rarely paid their bills. Again, this was the opposite of everything for which the professional journalism movement stood.[35]

## The Society Journalism Clubs

While bohemian clubs were popular in the last part of the nineteenth century, at the opposite end of the scale, society journalism clubs also existed. The society journalism clubs existed for the purpose of rubbing shoulders with others who were well off in the journalism business, being established exclusively in large cities, with the most well-known of the society press clubs in Chicago and New York City. Often the members included the publishers of large newspapers and only the most prominent members of the journalism community.[36] Fitting for a group that considered themselves a part of high society, these club meetings often offered multiple course feasts featuring French cuisine. Their guest speakers sometimes came from afar, even including the British author Charles Dickens.[37]

The New York Press Club was the first society press club or press club of any kind, founded in 1851 by *New York Times* editor Henry Raymond, the year that newspaper was founded. Sometimes it met at a famous high society restaurant called Delmonico's in what today is lower Manhattan, New York. Delmonico's was the first fine dining restaurant in the United States and is still in operation. At other times the New York Press Club met at the famous Astor House. Owned by a wealthy New York family, the Astor House was

---

[35] Norma Green, Stephen Lacy and Jean Folkerts, "Chicago Journalists at the Turn of the Century: Bohemians All?" *Journalism Quarterly* 66 (Winter 1989): 813, 821; *Chicago Press Club: Official Reference Book of the Press Club of Chicago Oldest Press Club in the World* (Chicago: Press Club of Chicago, 1922), 1.

[36] Augustus Maverick, *Henry D. Raymond and the New York Press for Thirty Years: Progress of American Journalism from 1840 To 1870* (Hartford, CT: A. S. Hale and Company, 1870), 328-9; John Weeks Moore, *Historical Notes on Printers and Printing 1420 To 1886* (Concord, MA: Republican Press Association, 1886), 253; Hudson, *Journalism in the United States*, 665.

[37] Banning, "Not Quite Professional," 3; John Thomas Scharf, *History of Saint Louis City and County: From the Earliest Periods to the Present Day* (Philadelphia: L. H. Everts, 1883), 958; Hudson, *Journalism in the United States*, 665.

one of the largest and best hotels in New York City. The New York Press Club speakers were the toast of the town, including European politicians and writers. However, the club was never considered to be professional and the conversations were secret, as there were no agendas or minutes.[38]

The society clubs had one element that was like the professional journalism clubs in that they believed journalism was an important occupation. However, there were stark differences between the two. The society crowd clubs were not interested in professionalization or helping society in a way that did not benefit themselves financially. This was probably because the society club members were already prominent in the community and saw no need to climb to a higher status. On the other hand, rural publishers populated the state press associations, and they personally would have benefitted status-wise from journalism being recognized as a profession.[39]

## Pushing Press Freedom to Promote Professionalization

Despite the people who pushed back against being called professionals, the professional ideal continued to be attractive to many journalists. This was reflected in annual publishers' association meetings, where journalism standards were discussed. The meetings included proposals of codes of ethics, essentially standards of work addressing problems which were causing the public to lose faith in newspapers. While some of the state publishers' associations pushed the message of professionalization in their annual meetings, the Missouri Press Association was more focused on this than others. In one 1868 Missouri Press Association speech, publisher Norman Colman said truth was vital for a newspaper to have credibility, noting: "But if [a newspaper is] untruthful, reckless statements and assertions are published as truthful, the tone of the public mind is gradually debased,

---

[38] Hudson, *Journalism in the United States*, 660, 666; Maverick, *Henry J. Raymond and the New York Press*, 328;

[39] F. O. Bennett, *History of the Press Club of Chicago* (Chicago: H.O. Shepard & Co., Printers, 1888), 3; John J. McPhaul, *Deadlines and Monkeyshines: The Fabled World of Chicago Journalists* (Englewood Cliffs, NJ.: Prentice-Hall, 1962), 150; *Press Club of Chicago: Official Reference Book of the Press Club of Chicago Oldest Press Club in the World* (Chicago: Press Club of Chicago, 1922), 2.

[and] becomes as familiar with falsehood as with truth, and pays but little credence to anything that is published."[40]

Another Missouri Press Association member John Marmaduke noted in 1871: "We conceive the mission of the Press to be to elevate, not debase; to enlighten, not darken; to instruct, not deceive; to inform, not mislead; to disseminate good, not evil; to propagate truth, not error, — in general, to... bear us on to a higher destiny."[41] Marmaduke came by his flowery language honestly as he had studied in Europe as well as at Harvard and Yale, and was also respected in Missouri as a Civil War hero.[42]

Other state press associations also identified as professionals, particularly in Wisconsin, Maine, Michigan and Minnesota. The Wisconsin Press Association held an organizational meeting in 1853, in which they called themselves professionals, and is the earliest example of a state press association identifying itself as professional, even before the organization's first full meeting in 1857. Similarly, the Maine Press Association began in 1864 and members strongly identified as professionals at that time and were familiar with the elements of professionalization. The Michigan Press Association also strongly identified as professionals from their 1868 founding, when they expressed concern regarding a need for ethics and university education.[43] Minnesota started a press association early on as well, the Minnesota Editors and Publishers Association emerging in 1867. At first, they were not interested in professionalism at all, as their first order of business focused on advertising and other business aspects of newspapers. However, in the 1880s they began to concentrate more on

---

[40] Norman J. Colman, "May 19, 1869 Annual Missouri Press Association Address," in J. W. Barrett, ed., *History and Transactions of the Editors and Publishers Association of Missouri* (Canton, MO: Canton Press Print, 1876), 23.

[41] John Marmaduke, "May 27, 1872 Annual Missouri Press Association Address," in J. W. Barrett, ed., *History and Transactions of the Editors and Publishers Association of Missouri* (Canton, MO: Canton Press Print, 1876), 73.

[42] W. L. Webb, *Battles and Biographies of Missourians or the Civil War Period of Our State*, 2 vols., 2nd ed. (Kansas City, Mo.: Hudson-Kimberly Publishing Company, 1903), 311; Floyd Calvin Shoemaker, *Missouri and Missourians: Land of Contrast and People of Achievement,* vol. 2 (Chicago: Lewis Publishing Company, 1943), 96, 106.

[43] Stephen A. Banning, "Fully Conscious of Their Power: Nineteenth Century Michigan Editors Search for Journalistic Professionalism," *American Journalism* 36, no. 3 (Fall 2019): 1-24.

journalism as a profession after one of the members complained the organization was spending too much time on sight-seeing vacation trips.[44]

These state press clubs were the vanguard of the journalism professionalization movement. As the nineteenth century progressed, efforts were made to move toward the elements of professionalism that doctors, lawyers and the clergy had set out, including the aforementioned university education and a widely used code of ethics.[45]

In the twentieth century, the newspaper institutions established by the Penny Press had been in place for almost three-quarters of a century, and the sensationalism that street sales encouraged was at an all-time high. In contrast, newspaper credibility was at a new low as newspapers tried to outdo each other with unbelievable and often untrue headlines, containing stories that were often high on excitement but low on believability. The concept that the press should be a guardian of democracy was in serious trouble.[46]

The Yellow Journalism Era was followed by the Muckrakers, who were investigative reporters usually working for magazines. The word muckrake came from the book *Pilgrim's Progress* by John Milton, in which it was used to describe a man who stirred foul smelling manure with a stick and never looked anywhere but down at the fertilizer. While this term was first used by United States President Theodore Roosevelt against investigative journalists as a slur, implying that they could only see bad things and nothing good, journalists took it as a badge of honor.[47]

The Muckrakers were fearless, with courage to speak truth to power, confronting wealthy institutions and exposing corruption. This period of time when society was concerned about cleaning up corruption and bad actors was called the Progressive Era, and it was partly fueled by muckraking

---

[44] Lee, *The Daily Newspaper in America*, 123-4; Stephen A. Banning, "The Maine Press Association Takes a Stand," *Maine Historical Journal*, Forthcoming; Banning, "The Professionalization of Journalism," 157; Dicken-Garcia, *Journalistic Standards in Nineteenth Century America*, 257.

[45] Stephen A. Banning, "Press Clubs Champion Journalism Education," in *Journalism 1908: Birth of a Profession,* ed. Betty Winfield (Columbia, MO: University of Missouri Press, 2008), 65.

[46] Douglas Birkhead, "The Power in the Image: Professionalism and the Communications Revolution," *American Journalism* 1, no. 2 (Winter 1984): 3.

[47] Fred J. Cook, *The Muckrakers: Crusading Journalists who Changed America* (Garden City, NY: Doubleday, 1972), 11.

articles which attacked institutions such as the Standard Oil refining monopoly, the meat packing industry and the patent medicine industry. One muckraking article called "The Brass Check" written in 1919 by Upton Sinclair, the author of the muckraking book *The Jungle*, attacked newspapers for a lack of ethics.[48]

## Good from Bad

The beginning of the twentieth century was a perfect storm of bad publicity for newspapers, and much of it came from the product itself, as many articles were petty, sexual, violent and considered obstructive to society. However, it created an opportunity for journalistic professionalization advocates to step forward.[49]

One of those advocates was Walter Williams, a member of the Missouri Press Association that pushed for a new kind of journalist. Williams saw future journalists as being university educated, belonging to a professional association and following a code of ethics, the professional dream that had been repeated in state press associations for half a century. Therefore, the Missouri Press Association became the impetus behind a journalism education proposal which petitioned the University of Missouri Board of Curators to open the world's first school of journalism. Williams led the charge. He was a Columbia, Missouri, newspaper editor who also happened to be a member of the University of Missouri Board of Curators. As a former president of the Missouri Press Association and National Editorial Association, he was in the perfect position to promote journalism education.[50]

In 1908, the first university school of journalism opened its doors at the University of Missouri in Columbia, Missouri. The school taught university courses in reporting, but also had a working newspaper which acted as a laboratory where students could practice. This was to satisfy the old timers,

---

[48] Upton Sinclair, *The Jungle* (New York: Doubleday, Page & Company, 1906).

[49] Michael Schudson, *Discovering the News* (New York: Basic Books, Inc., Publishers, 1978), 153; Marion Tuttle Marzolf, *Civilizing Voices: American Press Criticism 1880-1950* (New York: Longman Publishing Group, 1991), 14.

[50] Stephen A. Banning, "Press Clubs Champion Journalism Education," in *Journalism 1908: Birth of a Profession,* ed. Betty Winfield (Columbia, MO: University of Missouri Press, 2008), 65-81.

the practical printers, who felt the newspaper business could not be taught anywhere but in an actual newsroom.[51]

Williams became dean of the school when it opened, and proved to be an inspiring choice, as he was passionate about journalism ethics and he made it an important part of the curriculum. Later Williams was appointed president of the university, a surprising journey for someone who had been orphaned at age 14 and never had the financial wherewithal to attend college himself. However, Williams was as proud as a new father of the journalism school, explaining: "The new education for journalism differs from the old in that it recognizes journalism as a profession, as law and medicine are professions."[52]

A few years later, a second school of journalism commenced. The school of journalism at New York City's Columbia University launched in 1912, the result of an endowment in Joseph Pulitzer's will. These two journalism schools started slowly, but with the aid of passionate faculty, soon made a name for themselves as the quality of journalism students who graduated imparted credence to the belief that the school of journalism experiment was a success.[53]

With university schools of journalism underway, journalists worldwide began to discuss journalism education. Williams was a part of many of these discussions and grew increasingly concerned that journalists were misunderstanding journalism education's foundation. Williams saw ethics as the bedrock of the journalism education process, and while Williams saw the lab-style method as adequate for basic skills pedagogy, he viewed ethics instruction as schooling students in responsible journalism. To remind people of this, he created a code of ethics in 1914 known as the Journalist's Creed.[54]

The Journalist's Creed is not well known today, preceding the better known Canons of Journalism and Sigma Delta Chi's code of ethics. The creed itself

---

[51] Stephen A. Banning, "The Cradle of Professional Journalistic Education in the Mid-Nineteenth Century," *Journalism History Monographs* 4, no. 1 (2000) [Online serial]. http://www.scripps.ohiou.edu/mediahistory.

[52] James Melvin Lee, *History of American Journalism* (New York: Garden City Publishing Co., Inc., 1923), 661.

[53] Ronald T. Farrar, *A Creed for My Profession: Walter Williams, Journalist to the World* (Columbia, MO: University of Missouri Press, 1998), 157; Richard Terrill Baker, *A History of the Graduate School of Journalism Columbia University* (New York: Columbia University Press, 1954), 81.

[54] Farrar, *A Creed for My Profession*, 200.

was cast in bronze and displayed for many years at the Washington, D. C., National Press Club. It covered the standards of journalism that the Missouri Press Club had taught and published in their annual meetings for decades during the nineteenth century. None knew them better than Williams who, at 25 years old, had been the Missouri Press Association's youngest president. The standards included freedom of the press, truth telling, fairness, representation of society and independence (against bribery).[55]

## Professional Associations in the 20th Century

As previously stated, there had been professional associations in the nineteenth century, starting with the Maine Press Association in 1853.[56] However, in 1909, just a year after the first university school of journalism was founded, a new journalism association began, established by ten journalism students at Indiana's DePauw University. The DePauw University students called this Sigma Delta Chi, although the name was later changed to the Society of Professional Journalists. Sigma Delta Chi formed as a fraternity that quickly gained popularity.[57]

In 1922, editors met to form a professional organization called the American Society of Newspaper Editors (ASNE), and begin the work of creating a code of ethics. This organization was started by a group of high-ranking editors from large city newspapers, and while there was already a national organization for high ranking editors and publishers that dealt with business concerns (The American Newspaper Publishers Association), there was no similar organization focusing on ethics. The catalyst for the organization's formation was two articles published in the magazine the *Atlantic Monthly*, which were a scorching criticism of newspapers and the people who worked for them.[58]

One editor who read the articles became angry and decided to form a group that would closely examine journalism ethics. He met with several other editors at the Blackstone Hotel in Chicago and not long after, the first

---

[55] Sara Lockwood Williams, *Twenty Years of Education for Journalism* (Columbia, MO: E. W. Stephens Publishing Co., 1929), 3.
[56] Banning, "The Maine Press Association Takes a Stand," *Maine Historical Journal*, Forthcoming.
[57] Charles C. Clayton, *Sigma Delta Chi: Fifty Years of Freedom* (Carbondale, IL: Southern Illinois University Press, 1959), 43.
[58] Harvey Saalberg, "The Canons of Journalism: A 50 Year Perspective," *Journalism Quarterly* 5, no. 4 (1973): 731.

meeting of the ASNE was held. Once it formed, the members wasted no time in working on a code of ethics.[59] Much of it drawn from standards promoted by state press associations for almost seventy years.[60]

## Journalism Codes of Ethics in the 20th Century

A year after the ASNE launched they put out a code of ethics known as the Canons of Journalism. It had seven elements: 1) responsibility, 2) freedom of the press, 3) independence, 4) sincerity, truthfulness and accuracy, 5) impartiality, 6) fair play and 7) decency.[61] We will examine these elements closely in later chapters, as the Canons of Journalism distilled what was seen as ethical journalism at the time.

Three years after ASNE published a code of ethics, Sigma Delta Chi also created a code of ethics and published it. The 1926 Sigma Delta Chi code was essentially the same as the ASNE code in naming the basic elements of ethical journalism.[62]

The ASNE was originally only for editors from large newspapers in big cities, with the rules stating that editors had to live in a city with a population of at least 100,000 people, which meant journalists from smaller cities and newspapers were not welcome. While the ASNE and Sigma Delta Chi served different members, they both had an interest in promoting journalism ethics and the importance of journalism standards was solidified on a national level.[63]

---

[59] Paul Alfred Pratte, *Gods Within the Machine: A History of the American Society of Newspaper Editors, 1923-1993* (Westport, CT: Praeger, 1995), 2.

[60] Stephen A. Banning, "Truth is Our Ultimate Goal," *American Journalism* 16, no. 1 (Winter 1999): 17-39.

[61] Charles L. Allen, *Canons of Journalism, Adopted by the American Society of Newspaper Editors in Convention 1925* [sic] (Urbana, IL: University of Illinois Studio Press, 1928), 1; Pratte, *Gods Within the Machine,* 2; See also: Alice Fox Pins, *Read All About It: 50 Years of ASNE* (n. p.: American Society of Newspaper Editors, 1974).

[62] Bostrom, Bert. *Talent, Truth and Energy: Society of Professional Journalists Sigma Delta Chi.* (Chicago: Society of Professional Journalists, 1984), vi; Stephen A. Banning, "Truth is Our Ultimate Goal"; William Meharry Glenn, *The Sigma Delta Chi Story: 1909-1949* (Coral Gables, FL: Glade House, 1949).

[63] Clifford Christians, "Enforcing Media Codes," *Journal of Mass Media Ethics 1,* no. 1 (Fall/Winter 1985-6): 1.

## Discussion Questions

1. Remember: Can you identify the criteria for professionalization and the impetus behind journalism's involvement with professionalization?

2. Understand: What are the implications of not having a journalism code of ethics in communication for businesses, citizens and the communicators?

3. Apply: What do you find online when you search for instances in the last six months of ethical lapses in journalism? What stakeholders did it harm and what are the consequences of the breach, including to society as a whole?

4. Evaluate: As an administrator in a journalism business, how would you respond to a situation in which a reporter had engaged in a gross breach of what you consider to be ethical journalism? What consequences would there be and what actions would you take, including publishing a correction?

5. Create: Using the above situation, create a page of guidelines that describe the procedure for dealing with a perceived breach of ethics, including responses to the employee, other staff members and the public. What are completing concerns that you must balance in creating this document?

# CHAPTER FOUR

# THE FIRST JOURNALISM CODES OF ETHICS

This chapter examines the first widely used journalism code of ethics that came about in the twentieth century, looking at the pressure journalists were under, and why they decided to publicly endorse a code of ethics. It also examines the roots of the ethical principles that became the seven elements in the Canons of Journalism, which originated from press association standards of work many years before. This examination of the development of journalistic standards of work and loose codes of ethics into an accepted code that was then widely adopted, reveals the nearly half a century of thought and discussion that went into creating the Canons of Journalism. The intellectual ferment indicates this was the culmination of decades of deliberation.[1]

The Bill of Rights had claimed that free speech was a right in 1791 and the First Industrial Revolution created the ability to greatly increase printing production. After that, newspaper editors demonstrated that free speech without limits could seriously damage the government, society and newspaper credibility itself.[2] During this time in the first few years of the new republic, laws had been enacted limiting what could be printed. For instance, there were laws which said you could not undermine the government, a crime called sedition, which seemed to contradict the right to free speech and specifically the right to criticize government leaders.[3]

Another legal area which affected printers and publishers in the nineteenth century was libel law. The first widespread consideration of libel law in the last part of the nineteenth century was considered dangerous to free speech by some but welcomed by others. Before libel laws were passed, however, those who took umbrage with newspaper reports had another recourse, as in

---

[1] Stephen A. Banning, "Truth is Our Ultimate Goal," *American Journalism* 16, no. 1 (Winter 1999): 17.

[2] Leonard W. Levy, *Origin of the Bill of Rights* (New Haven, CT: Yale University Press), 43.

[3] Edwin Emery and Michael Emery, *The Press and America: An Interpretive History of the Mass Media*, 4th ed. (Englewood Cliffs, NJ: Prentice-Hall, 1984), 104.

the first half of the nineteenth century it was common for individuals insulted in a newspaper to challenge the printer to a duel even when the newspaper was printing the truth. The offended person was often a politician. Nevertheless, the printer was still required to duel with the offended person or back down, and it was common for a printer to have been involved with more than one duel. While this was originally seen as the civilized way to handle being slighted, opinions on dueling began to change, with laws being enacted that made the activity illegal. Privately, however, practices were instituted to avoid a dueling survivor's arrest. Because of the prevalence of dueling, at one time near St. Louis, Missouri, there was an island in the Mississippi River that was not in any legal jurisdiction, and so individuals went there to duel without fear of arrest. However, eventually libel laws were seen as a more civilized approach to restoring the dignity of someone who had been slighted, and as a result, dueling became passé.[4]

Despite some libel laws, a century after the First Amendment was ratified, the press was relatively unfettered by regulation. Nevertheless, some individuals were apprehensive about the behavior of the press at the beginning of the twentieth century, because Yellow Journalism had demonstrated that new limits were needed.[5]

The beginning of the twentieth century was also a time when many areas of society were under close scrutiny. Magazine journalists began to investigate corrupt areas of society, showing that a lack of regulation had allowed unscrupulous people to take advantage of others. Because people were upset by the articles, politicians acted. One area mentioned earlier in this book was patent medicines, but another area that a muckraker wrote about was the meat packing industry. Upton Sinclair wrote a book called *The Jungle*, revealing how unhealthy slaughter houses were and moving the government to regulate the meat packing industry. During this Progressive Era individuals also thought the press needed regulation, but journalists fought back, claiming it would undermine with the First Amendment.[6]

---

[4] Lawrence O. Christensen, William E. Foley, and Gary Kremer, eds., *Dictionary of Missouri Biography* (Columbia, MO: University of Missouri Press, 1999), 35, 66, 335, 446, 505.
[5] David R. Spencer, *The Yellow Journalism: The Press and America's Emergence as a World Power* (Evanston, IL: Northwestern University Press, 2007), 4.
[6] Linda Lawson, *Truth in Publishing: Federal Regulation of the Press's Business Practices, 1880-1920* (Carbondale, IL: SIU Press, 1993), 59.

# The Era of Change

The foundation of university schools of journalism, professional journalism associations and communication codes of ethics all transpired in the Progressive Era. The Progressive Era reformers believed the societal changes instigated by the First Industrial Revolution had been unchecked for too long. Individuals were open to change, making it an ideal period for journalists to establish a professional emphasis.[7]

At one time it was believed that the Canons of Journalism had been invented from scratch by the American Society of Newspaper Editors and Sigma Delta Chi. However, later research revealed that the Canons of Journalism borrowed heavily from nineteenth century standards of work and codes of ethics promoted by press associations starting right after the Civil War.[8] The fact that Walter Williams' Journalists Creed, the ASNE Canons of Journalism and the Sigma Delta Chi Code of ethics all occurred within a few years of each other and basically restated the same elements indicates that even among different groups of journalists at the time, there was a consensus regarding journalism standards.

As mentioned earlier, this chapter looks at the specific elements in the Canons of Journalism and why they were seen as important in the 1920s, when they were adopted and became popular. The seven Canons of Journalism elements emphasized 1) responsibility, 2) freedom of the press, 3) independence, 4) sincerity, truthfulness, accuracy, 5) impartiality, 6) fair play and 7) decency.[9] The remainder of the chapter will focus on an examination of the individual Canons of Journalism as they were viewed when they were adopted by the American Society of Newspaper Editors in 1923.

## Canon One: Responsibility

The first element in the Canons of Journalism is responsibility, a good start for this code of ethics because it is the foundation of journalism and was seen as touching everything a journalist does. The concept of responsible

---

[7] Richard Hofstadtler, *The Age of Reform: From Bryan to F.D.R.* (New York: Vintage Books, 2011), 191.

[8] Stephen A Banning, "Truth is Our Ultimate Goal," *American Journalism* 16, no. 1 (Winter 1999): 17-39.

[9] Paul Alfred Pratte, *Gods Within the Machine: A History of the American Society of Newspaper Editors, 1923-1993* (Westport, CT: Praeger, 1995), 205-6.

journalism is a consequence of Enlightenment ideas, specifically Immanuel Kant's deontological ethics.[10] The word deontological comes from the Greek word duty, and responsibility was the word usually used by nineteenth century editors to describe journalistic duty.[11]

There must be duty in journalism because freedom of speech is a right, and therefore there is a corresponding responsibility. Specifically, in journalism this responsibility was seen as producing content that helps society, and in a democratic context, allowing for an informed electorate. Obviously, many journalists neglected this concept, as Yellow Journalism had clearly spelled out what irresponsible journalism could be. As discussed in previous chapters, in the case of Yellow Journalism, journalists were publishing only the bloodiest crimes, the most scandalous of relationships and the most sensational stories, and items that had to do with keeping democracy alive did not fit into the Yellow Journalism agenda.[12]

Yellow Journalism was not an expected problem at the First Amendment's inception, as the past threat had been from a censoring monarchy. The Bill of Rights' creators had little experience with the problems of a free press, because one had never before existed. Yellow Journalism also made it clear that there had to be some limits to free speech.[13] In allowing a libertine approach to free speech, others' rights to truthful information were being destroyed. This same kind of clash of rights had occurred with medicine and food distribution, and the answer for these two challenges to the Constitution had been government regulation. Journalists have almost always been in opposition with the idea of impeding the First Amendment and those in the early twentieth century hoped the answer was in journalists' understanding responsibility, particularly though a code of ethics.[14]

---

[10] Victoria S. Wike, *Kant on Happiness in Ethics* (Albany, NY: State University of New York Press, 1994), 111.

[11] Bill Kovach and Tom Rosentiel, *The Elements of Journalism: What Newspeople Should Know and the Public Should Expect* (New York: Crown Publishers, 2001), 179.

[12] Frank Luther Mott, *American Journalism: A History of Newspapers in the United States Through 250 Years 1690 to 1940* (New York: Macmillan Company, 1941), 549.

[13] Emily Erickson, "Yellow Journalism," in *Encyclopedia of American Journalism*, ed. Stephen L. Vaughn (New York: Routledge, 2008), 608; Sidney Kobre, *The Yellow Press and the Gilded Age* (Tallahassee, FL: Florida State University, 1964), 325.

[14] Edward J. Whetmore, *Mediamerica: Form, Content and Consequence of Mass Communication* (Belmont, CA: Wadsworth Publishing Company, 1982), 50.

The concept of journalistic responsibility in the early twentieth century came from mindsets that had formed over the previous several decades, when press associations in the nineteenth century had talked about standards. Then muckraker Upton Sinclair had written "The Brass Check," admonishing journalists what not to do; Walter Williams, the product and promoter of press associations himself, had written "The Journalist's Creed" to emphasize ethics; famous columnist Walter Lippmann, had written the book *Public Opinion* about the role of the journalist in society, and that the journalist was vital to keeping the United States free.[15] These ideas of responsibility were all rooted in the First Amendment and the reasoning behind it, which included a marketplace of ideas where individuals could hear many viewpoints and select the truth. It included the notion that free speech was indispensable to keep the government in check, and the electorate informed. Therefore, the prevailing perspective was that it was the press's job to observe the government and provide different viewpoints to the populace, a factor that academic and former journalist J. Herbert Altschull in *Agents of Power* called the "democratic assumption."[16]

Understanding what would happen without responsible journalism also helps us understand what responsible journalism is. The picture of a state without free speech and responsible journalism is one where no information systems provide different ideas, and no one can criticize the government. In such a system, the individuals who vote would not have the information to make sage decisions. Furthermore, if the government controlled the news, elections would be a fraud and the public would not remove ineffective leaders because the public would not know the leaders had performed poorly, and democracy would fail.[17]

The consequence is that individuals need accurate news to vote with political acumen, the foundation for the right to know. While privacy laws say that people do not have the right to know everything, the public does have the right to know enough about the government to make good voting decisions, and if news and free speech did not exist, we would have no need

---

[15] See Upton Sinclair, *The Brass Check* (Pasadena, CA: Self, 1919); Ronald T. Farrar, A *Creed for My Profession: Walter Williams, Journalist to the World* (Columbia, MO: University of Missouri Press, 1998); Walter Lippmann, *Public Opinion* (New York: Harcourt, Brace and Company, Inc., 1922), 299.

[16] J. Herbert Altschull, *Agents of Power* (White Plains, NY: Longman, 1984), 190.

[17] Gerald C. Stone, Mary K. O'Donnell, and Stephen Banning, "Public Perceptions of Newspaper's Watchdog Role," *Newspaper Research Journal* 18, no. 1-2 (January 1997): 86.

for elections, because we would not be in a democracy. Some individuals think that democracy means being able to vote, however, it also means having free speech so that individuals can hear the truth about the government in order to vote responsibly.[18]

The Canons of Journalism define responsibility simply, stating that responsibility has to do with motivations. It says money is not a problem as long as it is not the journalist's main goal, which is to serve people. This is a general statement that can be taken many ways, although it is followed by the rest of the seven Canons of Journalism, and these other elements are more specific and further define what responsibility meant when the Canons of Journalism were written. The Canons of Journalism's defining goal of journalism as serving others could be construed as a communitarian goal, which sees the duty of the press as helping the community.[19]

While Yellow Journalism at the end of the nineteenth century made people realize a change was needed, state press club editors and publishers had been concerned about a lack of responsibility before that. Three state press associations in Missouri, Michigan, and Maine, were especially interested in ethics in the second half of the nineteenth century, and their association records contain the first recorded discussions of journalism ethics and standards.[20] As far back as 1869, only four years after the Civil War, Missouri editor Norman Colman said, "Like all other professions the Editor has grave and responsible duties devolving on it."[21] In the same speech to other editors, Colman asked, "What other profession is of equal

---

[18] Magda Konieczna, *Journalism Without Profit: Making News when the Market Fails* (New York: Oxford University Press, 2018), 9.
[19] Clifford G. Christians, John P. Ferre and P. Mark Fackler, *Good News: Social Ethics and the Press* (New York: Oxford University Press, 1993), 14.
[20] Stephen A. Banning, "Unearthing the Origin of Journalistic Professionalization in the Mid-nineteenth Century" (Master's thesis, University of Missouri, 1993); Stephen A. Banning, "The Professionalization of Journalism: A Nineteenth- Century Beginning," *Journalism History* 24, no. 4 (Winter 1998-1999): 157-60; Stephen A. Banning, "The Maine Press Association Takes a Stand: Promoting Professional Identity in the Nineteenth Century," *Maine Historical Journal,* Forthcoming; Stephen A. Banning, "Fully Conscious of Their Power: Nineteenth Century Michigan Editors Search for Journalistic Professionalism," *American Journalism* 36, no. 3 (Fall 2019): 1-24.
[21] Norman J. Colman, "May 19, 1869 Annual Missouri Press Association Address," in *History and Transactions of the Editors and Publishers Association of Missouri: 1867-1876,* ed. J. W. Barrett (Canton, MO: Canton Press Print, 1876), 21.

responsibility?"[22] There were few people at the time who were more qualified than Colman to talk about professionalism, and the classic professions, which were doctors, lawyers and the clergy. Colman had experience with two of these, as he had a law license and had trained to be a member of the clergy.[23] It might seem strange that this talk of the importance of journalistic responsibility happened so long before the Canons of Journalism were adopted in 1923. However, the Constitution was not that old in 1869, when Colman spoke, and the First Amendment was just under 80 years old. We tend to see democracy in the United States today as indestructible. However, a hundred and fifty years ago it was still seen as an experiment that needed help for it to succeed, as in the nineteenth century democratic government was seen as test that could fail.

Another Missouri journalist, C. B. Wilkinson explained that democracy was what gave journalists power but that it was also the pillar of their responsibility. Wilkinson explained in 1868, "Democratic, the newspaper surely is, for it bears alike to the hovel of the poor to the palace of the lordly and the loyally rich, the faithful record of every day's transactions."[24] The important part of these statements and the freedom of speech element in the Canons of Journalism is that the journalist's responsibility is to society above selfish motives.

The Missouri Press Association's John Marmaduke had gone to Harvard and Yale, and was familiar with Enlightenment philosophy which advocated the common person's nobility. Both his father and great grandfather had been governors and he had been a Major-General in the Civil War. During the Civil War, Marmaduke had been through several battles, had been wounded in action and had even been held as a prisoner of war.[25] In short, Marmaduke was the kind of person of whom others took note. He advised editors at the 1873 annual Missouri Press Association meeting that the press was doing good things: "It is doing more to disseminate knowledge and to educate people up to a certain standard and at less expense than all other

---

[22] Colman, *History and Transactions*, 21.

[23] Coleman would also become the first United States Secretary of Agriculture. At the time Colman spoke to the Missouri Press Association, he was founder and editor of the *Missouri Ruralist*, a newspaper that continues today in digital form on the Internet.

[24] C. B. Wilkinson, "May 24, 1868 Annual Missouri Press Association Address," in *History and Transactions*, 8.

[25] Fellow Missouri editor J. C. Moore had served under him during the Civil War.

instrumentalities of the age."[26]

Marmaduke believed it was the press' responsibility to keep a close eye on the government. He stated: "By its [the press'] vigilance and omnipresence Tyranny is anticipated, and its purpose defeated."[27] In modern times, this is referred to as the watchdog role of the press.[28]

Missouri editor William Switzler also saw the watchdog role as important. In 1876 at the annual Missouri Press Association meeting, he declared: "It [the press] is theoretically and ought to be practically, an honest and sleepless sentinel of the watchtower of their liberties, and a guardian of their special interests, industries and activities whatever they may be."[29]

Like Missouri, Michigan had a state press association interested in professionalism, and during their annual meeting in 1883 guest speaker Elijah Melville Stone spoke about ethics and responsibility in journalism. Stone was a prominent journalist and lawyer who had founded the *Chicago Daily News*. Stone told the Michigan editors: "Now in common fairness, if not in ethics, are we not bound to recognize the responsibilities growing out of this position of influence and power we occupy?"[30] Stone clearly believed it was this responsibility which required journalists to have ethics.

Maine also had a state press association in the 1800s that was very interested in both professionalization and ethics. For instance, in 1881 Maine editor B. P. Snow explained: "The responsibility of caring for the moral education the highest of all cannot be wholly shifted from the shoulders of the journalist to those of other professions."[31] In addition to the word responsibility, Maine reporters talked of their duty to society, and in 1882

---

[26] John Marmaduke, "May 27, 1873 Annual Missouri Press Association Address," in *History and Transactions*, 71.

[27] Marmaduke, *History and Transactions*, 72.

[28] Stone, O'Donnell, and Banning, "Public Perceptions of Newspaper's Watchdog Role," 86.

[29] William Switzler, "June 6, 1876, Annual Missouri Press Association Address," in *History and Transactions*, 125.

[30] Elijah Stone, "The Model Newspaper," in *Michigan Press Association at the Sixteenth Annual Meeting Held at Detroit, March 29-30, 1883* (Nashville, MI: News Steam Print, 1883), 11.

[31] B. P. Snow, "The Newspaper Press," in *Eighteenth Annual Report of the Maine Press Association for the Year Ending February 1, 1881*, ed. Joseph Wood (Skowhegan, ME: Joseph Wood, 6 Madison Street, 1881), 17.

editor Samuel Lane even gave a speech called "The Press: Its Power and Duty."[32]

## Canon Two: Freedom of the Press

While discussions had taken place as to what free speech was in the 1920s when the Canons were created, little Supreme Court action had occurred in the previous century. Speech seemed free, but there were limitations. One of the many examples of freedom of speech not being allowed occurred in the first part of the nineteenth century. Before the Civil War, abolitionists who aggressively opposed slavery had a problem in sending out their newspapers. The abolitionists wanted those in southern slaveholding states to receive them, but a federal law was enacted allowing states to refuse to deliver mail which was not legal in their state. Because anti-slavery newspapers were illegal in the south under the Post Office Act of 1836, any anti-slavery mail could be destroyed there. Sometimes mobs destroyed anti-slavery newspapers, as in Alton, Illinois, where the editor of an abolitionist newspaper, Elijah Lovejoy, was shot to death in 1837.[33]

One law in World War I did have an effect on free speech. The Espionage Act of 1917 made discussion of the government during wartime more dangerous. This act made discouraging people to buy war bonds, causing disloyalty, or promoting an enemy of the country, a crime, with the punishment of a fine of up to ten thousand dollars and a possible twenty-year prison sentence. This was a broad law and in peacetime might not have passed. However, because the U.S. population at the time was more afraid of the German army than the U.S. government, the law did not raise many eyebrows. In general, the laws affecting free speech leading up to the 1923 American Society of Newspaper Editors Canons of Journalism were few, and those that existed had generally not been good for journalism.[34]

Freedom of the press is important when understanding journalism. While the element of responsibility talks about what a journalist is obligated to do,

---

[32] Samuel W. Lane, "The Press, Its Power and Duty," in *Nineteenth Annual Report of the Proceedings of the Maine Press Association for the Year Ending, February 1, 1882*, ed. Joseph Wood (Bar Harbor, ME: Mount Desert Publishing Company, 1882), 15.

[33] Paul Simon, *Freedom's Champion: Elijah Lovejoy* (Carbondale, IL: Southern Illinois University Press, 1994), 155.

[34] Jeffery A. Smith, *War and Press Freedom: The Problem of Prerogative Power* (New York: The Oxford University Press, 1999), 39, 148.

freedom of the press is the reason journalists are able to do it, as it is an enabler of responsibility. By comparison, examples of press systems with less freedom are Russia and China.[35]

Freedom of speech is often taken for granted in the United States, but in reality, the United States was the first country to experiment with freedom of speech, and many other countries who practice it have copied the U.S. system. Even ancient Greece, the United States' template for democracy, did not practice free speech. For example, if speech had been free in Greece, the philosopher Socrates would not have been condemned to die for allegedly corrupting the young people of Athens by his words.[36]

Because free speech is what gives journalism its privileged position, it is carefully protected. If criticism of the government were removed, entertainment programs would continue, but everything reported about the government would be untrustworthy.

## Canon Three: Independence

According to the Canons of Journalism, independence means freedom from influences other than working for the public good, which is seen as the public having the information it requires as an assurance the government is operating in the people's interest. Specifically, the canon warns against promotion and partisanship, cautioning journalists not to promote anything that is paid for without enlightening the audience of that fact. In other words, an individual should not endorse a politician or product when they have secretly received a payment to do so, something that happened a great deal in the nineteenth century.[37]

Independence was one of the most difficult elements to follow when this canon was written because it cost so much to run a printing press. The press itself was expensive, as was the paper and ink. It was also a full-time job, and money had to come from somewhere. At times payment came from the

---

[35] Todd C. Helmus, Elizabeth Bodine-Baron, Andrew Radin, Madeline Magnuson, Joshua Mendelsohn, William Marcellino, Andriy Bega, and Zev Winkelman, *Russian Social Media Influence: Understanding Russian Propaganda in Eastern Europe* (N. p.: Rand Corporation, 2018), 7, 27.

[36] Arlene W. Saxonhouse, *Free Speech and Democracy in Ancient Athens* (New York: Cambridge University Press, 2006), 100.

[37] Hazel Dicken-Garcia, *Journalistic Standards in Nineteenth Century America* (Madison, WI: University of Wisconsin Press, 1989), 175.

government and political parties, as both demanded a say in what was printed. Sometimes income came from subscriptions, but many individuals could not afford a long-term subscription and others did not pay what they owed. This was also a hidden influence on a printer to publish popular opinions, because subscribers would stop paying if they did not like what they read. Street sales were the same way, in that the headlines had to attract, or there would be no sales and the printer would go out of business. Another way that editors received money was through advertising, which has always been a threat to independence, because if an advertiser does not like what the newspaper says, it may withdraw support as retribution, making reporters reticent to write negative articles about an advertiser.[38]

Today we call the mixture of advertising and editorials advertorials, a practice that was condemned in the nineteenth century by a speaker at the Maine Press Association. In 1874, editor Howard Owen gave a speech called "Advertising Rates and Ad Agencies" in which he said: "Let us encourage liberal and legitimate advertising, and set our faces against this strange and unwholesome admixture that neutralizes and compromises the honor and dignity of our profession."[39]

While newspapers became more independent of party support at the time of the Penny Press than they had been in the past, they were susceptible to business influence and influence from politicians who paid for recommendations in the editorial pages, a practice called paid puffs.[40] This was different than the term puffery that is used today, which means advertising exaggeration that individuals understand is false. For instance, if an advertisement says that a brand of toothpaste will change your life forever, most people realize this is an exaggeration and do not take it literally. Advertising with this kind of puffery is legal in the United States, even though it is not literally the truth. The puffs of the nineteenth century

---

[38] Bob Franklin and Mark Hanna, "Advertising," in *Key Concepts in Journalism Studies*, eds., Bob Franklin, Martin Hamer, Hark Hanna, Marie Kinsey, and John E. Richardson (Thousand Oaks, CA: Sage, 2005), 9.

[39] Howard Owen, "Advertising Rates and Agencies," in *Transactions of the Maine Editors and Publishers' Association, from 1870 To 1874, Inclusive,* ed. Joseph Wood (Wiscasset, ME: Printed by Joseph Wood, 1874), 29.

[40] Alfred McClung Lee, *The Daily Newspaper in America: The Evolution of a Social Instrument* (New York: The Macmillan Company, 1937), 320.

were different in that they were secret payments to editors for their endorsements, or what today we call advertorials.[41]

Many journalists in the nineteenth century thought the under the table payments for paid puffs were unethical and undermined the credibility of journalists, projecting an image to the world that the editor's opinions could be bought and paid for. For this reason, some editors viewed them as worse than a bribe. One of those editors was P. G. Ferguson, who wrote a poem about puffs in 1870, saying editors who took payment for puffs were traitors. Ferguson poetically slammed this group, saying of puffs: "This journal stooped, and like a mousing owl, sold its opinions with unblushing face and smeared its sacred robes with offal foul."[42]

Ferguson was not alone in his hatred of secret paid endorsements and in 1875, Missouri editor Mark DeMotte called out editors who accepted paid puffs saying: "To print paid personal puffs, as our own editorial or local opinion, is a prostitution of our paper wholly inexcusable; and if indulged in to any great extent, will bring the just contempt of the public upon us."[43] DeMotte added: "Our readers have a right to know whether what we say of the witness of a man for party nomination is our own belief or the drivel of a hired brain."[44]

The third item the canons warned against was partisanship. It is interesting that the canon did not say that the editor cannot endorse a candidate in an editorial and being partisan in an editorial was sometimes seen as acceptable because it was labeled as opinion and not presented as fact. However, the canon warns that the editor must still tell the truth, even in an editorial.[45]

The question of partisanship also reflects on the journalistic concept of objectivity. The history of objectivity in journalism indirectly goes back to the First Amendment, and the ideas from whence it came, including the Enlightenment Era. The idea of journalistic objectivity did not exist when

---

[41] Margaret Duffy and Esther Thorson, *Persuasion Ethics Today* (New York: Routledge, 2015), 4.
[42] P. G. Ferguson, "The Press," in *History and Transactions*, 58.
[43] Mark Demotte, "May 1875 Annual Missouri Press Association Address," in *History and Transactions*, 102.
[44] Demotte, "May 1875 Annual Missouri Press Association Address," in *History and Transactions*, 102.
[45] Pratte, *Gods Within the Machine*, 205-6.

the United States became a country and for the first four decades after the First Amendment was passed newspapers were bitterly partisan.[46]

Because of this, during the nineteenth century, Penny Press newspapers were criticized for not carrying politics. However, the idea of objectivity began to be seen as a positive one for democracy. An objective press was seen as a single press solution to the marketplace of ideas as it seemed there could not be a better manner in which to channel a multiplicity of political positions to the public than through this conduit. Therefore, objectivity came to be seen as a method for informing people about government and may be one of the ethical principles most associated with a professional journalist. The idea that a journalist can cover a story in such a way as to represent the interests of more than one party is now firmly seen as a tool for the formation of an informed electorate. [47]

Some journalists in the nineteenth century, were already concerned about this. In fact, more than forty years before the Canons of Journalism, in 1876, Missouri editor William Switzler articulated to Missouri Press Association members that editors needed a standard of conduct. Switzler stated that it was one-hundred years since the American War for Independence, and explained it was not a time for partisanship, noting: "Great and singular perils and strong temptations to bitter words and partisan excesses, will environ the press. Let us illustrate a royal virtue by resisting them . . . while we are sometimes partisans, we are always patriots."[48]

## Canon Four: Sincerity, Truthfulness and Accuracy

The idea behind sincerity, truthfulness and accuracy in the Canons of Journalism is that journalists should try their best to get the truth. This means doing whatever is possible to get the facts right, and the canon makes clear that not taking the time or effort to get the details right is no excuse for inaccuracy.[49]

The canon also makes a second point, that headlines should reflect the story. This was a result of the Penny Press method of selling newspapers on the street solely based on the main headline. The problem with this method was

---

[46] Dicken-Garcia, *Journalistic Standards in Nineteenth Century America*, 175.
[47] Stephen J. A. Ward, *The Invention of Journalism Ethics: The Path to Objectivity and Beyond,* 2nd ed. (Chicago: McGill-Queen's University Press, 2015), 336.
[48] Switzler, in *History and Transactions*, 131-3.
[49] Pratte, *Gods Within the Machine*, 206.

that the readers realized the deception as soon as they read the story and lowered their opinion of newspapers. Conversely, the writers of the Canons of Journalism, and many before them, felt that journalism should expose deception, not be a part of it.

In the 1800s state press associations talked about the importance of truth in reporting. Missouri editor Norman Colman advised the Missouri Press Association members: "It is always better to deal with facts and principles."[50] At another meeting, editor C. B. Wilkinson explained the importance of truth by admonishing: "In all matters of principle the voice of the editor should be the voice which truth and right send up from his soul . . .The newspaper scatters the mists of ignorance and prejudice by flooding the pathway of man with the sunlight of truth."[51]

One of the ways journalists in the past have arrived at truth and accuracy was through research. An example of this occurred just four years after the Civil War, when editor Nelson Dingly, Jr., explained at a Maine Press Association meeting that research was vital. He claimed: "This is indeed a profession requiring for the highest success, careful and thorough preparation."[52] Dingley's admonitions were mirrored in the Canons of Journalism more than a half century later which stated: "By every consideration of good faith, a newspaper is constrained to be truthful. It is not to be excused by a lack of thoroughness and accuracy within its control, or failure to obtain command of these essential qualities."[53]

## Canon Five: Impartiality

The canon on impartiality is clear about bias, and that it has no place in journalism. Again, as in the element of independence, it is clear that editorials labeled as opinion are allowed. However, the point is not to allow opinionated writing to be represented as news. In the Canons of Journalism, impartiality is different from partisanship in that partisanship is politically

---

[50] Norman Coleman, "May 19, 1869 Annual Missouri Press Association Address," in *History and Transactions*, 22.
[51] C. B. Wilkinson, "May 24, 1868 Annual Missouri Press Association Address," in *History and Transactions*, 13.
[52] Nelson Dingly, Jr. "Address," in *Transactions of the Editors and Publishers' Association of Maine* (Portland, ME: Monitor Printing Company, 1869), 17.
[53] Pratte, *Gods Within the Machine*, 206.

motivated and being impartial meant being fair in other things besides politics.

## Canon Six: Fair Play

In the Canons of Journalism, fair play addresses the idea that people who have been accused of something in the media, should have the right to defend themselves. The canon does not say that no one can be accused, but says those who are, should be given space for a response, which avoids a one-sided story. The canon also suggests caution in cases which are private matters, specifically noting that the public's curiosity is not necessarily the public's right to know.[54]

The canon also says the newspaper needs to make a public correction if it makes an error, and the correction needs to be done quickly and fully disclose the mistake, in that whereas mistakes are inevitable, prompt admission can help restore reader trust. While this element made it into the 1923 Canons of Journalism, it had concerned journalists in Michigan forty years before. Michigan Press Association speaker Elijah Melville Stone was firm that journalists be fair in their reporting, advising the Michigan journalists: "That which I do not believe in is careless, reckless, impertinent, and party journalism. It is a reproach to our profession."[55] Stone then defined careless journalists: "Having the power to do about as they please, and fully conscious of their power, they jump to conclusions and cut and slash, with little care as to whether their assault is just or unjust and utterly heedless to the consequences."[56]

## Canon Seven: Decency

Decency is not a word frequently used in a modern context. Therefore, this book will tend to discuss the subject the word referred to in the canons rather than the word decency itself. The call for decency in the Canons of Journalism referred to not publishing anything that appealed to base instincts. By this, the canon referred to the kind of stories that the Yellow Journalists often used, including the intimate details of violent crimes,

---

[54] Pratte, *Gods Within the Machine*, 206.
[55] Stone, in *Michigan Press Association*, 11, 12.
[56] Stone, in *Michigan Press Association*, 12.

stories of sex, etc.[57] This might seem prudish today, but in 1923 when the Canons of Journalism were adopted, the Yellow Journalism stories of sex, violence and sensationalism were still fresh in their minds. Additionally, the idea of decency as an element in a code of ethics had been discussed in state press association meetings many decades before, even before the Yellow Journalism Era. Speaking to the Maine Press Association in 1869, editor W. E. Stevens viewed decency as an important standard, opining: "We can never as a profession attain to that high standard which the influence we can command entitles us, until we cease to regard the journals we conduct as strainers, through which to filter our own petty likes and dislikes."[58] Decency was also a concern for journalist Elijah Melville Stone, when in 1883 he was the guest speaker at a Michigan Press Association gathering, castigating journalists who had fallen below its standard: "But mean and more despicable is the nasty journalist. Because his claim that his sheet is a newspaper gives him license to print those things which Anthony Comstock would step on if published in any other way, he besmears and beslimes our firesides with impunity."[59] Comstock was the man behind the Comstock Act of 1873, which condemned indecent writing.[60]

While the word decency may seem like an anachronism, the importance of the canon of decency should not be ignored in that it refers to remaining in the bounds of what society will accept, a principle the law refers to as community standards. However, the complication in comprehending journalistic decency is subjectivity, in that what was considered base conduct ten years ago, may seem mild by current standards. Furthermore, the difficulty expands exponentially when the Internet's global reach is

---

[57] W. Joseph Campbell, *Yellow Journalism: Puncturing the Myths, Defining the Legacies* (Westport, CT: Greenwood Publishing Group, 2001), 53.

[58] W. E. Stevens, "Journalism," in *Doings of the Editors & Publishers' Association of Maine at Biddleford, August 7 & 8, 1867* (Portland, ME: Printed by B. Thurston & Co., 1867), 20.

[59] Elijah Melville Stone, in *Michigan Press Association at the Sixteenth Annual Meeting Held at Detroit, March 29-30, 1883,* 12.

[60] The Comstock Act forbade sending obscene materials in the mail. Because many newspaper subscriptions were delivered by mail, it affected newspapers as well, although Comstock usually left mainstream newspapers alone. Paul S. Boyer, *Purity in Print: Book Censorship in America from the Gilded Age to the Computer Age* (Madison, WI: University of Wisconsin Press, 2002), 98; Andrea Friedman, *Prurient Interests: Gender, Democracy, and Obscenity in New York City, 1909-1945* (New York: Columbia University Press, 2000), 17.

factored in, and one considers that content created in New York City may be read in Dubai, where the standard of decency may be a culture apart.[61]

In the next three chapters the Canons of Journalism will continue to be examined. This time, however, it will focus on a more modern context, including additional thinking pertaining to journalism ethics that has taken place since the Canons of Journalism were adopted. This discussion will provide a foundation for understanding the framework for ethical guidelines in the past, which is essential for creating a code of ethics that applies to current technology.

## Discussion Questions

1. Remember: Can you identify the specific problems that the Canons of Journalism addressed?

2. Understand: What circumstances and problems led to the formation of the Canons of Journalism?

3. Apply: Which one (or more) of the problems addressed in the Canons of Journalism are extant in today's media?

4. Evaluate: Give one or more examples of media situations in the last year which violated at least one Canon of Journalism. Use a search engine and enter the key words "media fails."

5. Create: Look over the specific problems you listed in the first question above and try to think of one or more areas of ethical misconduct that might have been missed.

---

[61] Robert Trager, Susan Dente Ross, and Amy Reynolds, *The Law of Journalism and Mass Communication* (Thousand Oaks, CA: CQ Press, 2017), 446.

# CHAPTER FIVE

# TODAY'S PROBLEM OF CREDIBILITY PART 1: THE CANONS OF RESPONSIBILITY AND INDEPENDENCE

In this chapter the Canons of Journalism's elements of responsibility and independence are examined in relation to the time since the Canons of Journalism were adopted. These are the first and third elements in the Canons of Journalism. The second element, freedom of the press, is not being examined as it is less an action that journalists can perform and more a condition of being able to work. Chapter Four explored journalists' motivations in constructing the 1923 Canons of Journalism, and these elements are examined to ascertain if they are still indispensable in modern times.

## The Canons of Journalism: Responsibility

The canons claim public trust demands journalistic responsibility. In modern times this is referred to as credibility, which today is low for journalism in general.[1] An example of a lack of responsibility in communication can be seen in the work of video blogging star Logan Paul, who has made millions of dollars on his YouTube channel which has over eighteen million subscribers. However, Paul created a scandal when the public claimed he had gone too far in his search for interesting subjects to cover. Paul had taken his camera crew to a Japanese forest known for its large number of suicides, and proceeded to tape a standup video segment in front of the body of a woman who had committed suicide in the forest. Public outcry was quick, and Paul eventually apologized, illustrating that even when individuals providing information do not have high standards, the public

---

[1] Bill Kovach and Tom Rosenstiel, *The Elements of Journalism: What News People Should Know and Public Should Expect* (New York: Three Rivers Press, 2001), 66, 74.

still has expectations of responsibility.[2]

Another example of a lack of responsibility concerns one of the world's formerly largest and oldest newspapers. The history of the News of the World in London lasted over a century, epitomizing many of the kinds of journalism excesses the Canon's of Journalism were designed to limit. For this reason, we will spend time studying the rise of this financially successful newspaper and its ultimate demise. When John Browne Bell started the *News of the World*, he could not have imagined that his shoe string start up would last 168 years, or thought it would become the most distributed newspaper in the world. He probably also could not have imagined the kind of scandal that would bring it down a century and a half later. In 1843, Bell's mind was on something else entirely, as he was trying to decide how to profit from a new approach to newspapers being used in the United States.[3]

The Penny Press newspaper formula had begun only a decade before, and Bell pondered whether it might work in England. While the United States had a different culture, Bell imagined its success in England as well, and determined if a newspaper filled with stories of scandal spelled burgeoning riches in America, it would work in England too. Bell shrugged off the personal costs, as he had been a journalist previously, and he liked the business, perhaps too much for his wealthy father's liking, as he had disinherited him. Bell saw the new formula as a way to continue doing what he loved and a way to return to the comfortable style of living with which he had once been accustomed.[4]

The cost of the individual newspapers was a problem, as Bell knew he would have to make it affordable to the great masses of London. The challenge came not from the cost of printing, but from the reaction of newspaper distributing agents, who balked at selling a newspaper for only three pence.[5] Bell knew cheap presses had been tried before in London in

---

[2] Jonah Engel Bromwich, "Logan Paul, YouTube Video Star Says Posting of Suicide Video was 'Misguided,'" *New York Times,* January 2, 2018, https://www.nytimes.com/2018/01/02/business/media/logan-paul-youtube.html.
[3] James Mussell, "The Foundation and Early Years of the News of the World: 'Capacious Double Sheets,'" in *The News of the World and the British Press, 1843-2011*, ed. Laurel Brake, Chandrika Kaul and Mark W. Turner, 11-26. (New York: Palgrave Macmillan, 2016), 15.
[4] "News of the World: 1843-2011," *The Press Gazette*, July 8, 2011, www.pressgazett.co.uk/node/4758.
[5] "The News of the World's Sensational History," *The Guardian,* July 7, 2011, www.guardian.co.uk/media/2011/jul/07/news-of-the-world-history.

an attempt to capitalize on Day's idea with little success. However, those newspapers had been inferior sheets focusing on nothing more than the theater, so Bell won the argument with his agents and his newspaper soon sold for three pence.[6]

In some ways, Bell was far away from the scandal that would ultimately bring down his newspaper, but he was still responsible. After all, it was Bell who decided to follow the path of the Penny Press newspapers and feed his readers a steady diet of scandal in such a successful manner that the *News of the World* was soon the most widely circulated newspaper in the world. Newspapers like Bell's were ultimately the catalyst for journalism ethics, but the rules for journalists' ethical conduct had not been formed at the time he started. In fact, objectivity, which became a staple of twentieth century concepts of journalistic professionalism, was at that time considered a wise business choice rather than an ethical sacrifice.[7]

True to form, the *News of the World* would never change format, and from its heyday to its purchase by Rupert Murdoch in 1969 it was a sensational newspaper. It was the emphasis of income over ethics which ultimately led to the newspaper giant's demise in 2011. The fall of the *News of the World* was especially painful for journalism because it was one of the last remaining superstar newspapers, surviving the shifts of technology which closed many of its competitors. Some might see the closing as a tribute to the professional codes of the past which the tabloids like the *News of the World* had shunned.[8]

While the public were still drawn to gossip when the *News of the World* ceased publication in 2011 as much as it had when Bell founded the paper in 1843, it was not willing to let a newspaper threaten and bribe public officials in the way the *News of the World* was alleged to have done. It is difficult to comprehend why the public decided to draw the line on journalism excess with the hacking scandal, and whether it was because of a lower trust in media, or in spite of it. However, the public expected journalists to behave at some level of responsibility. The public was not

---

[6] Laurel Brake and Maryso Demour, eds., *Dictionary of Nineteenth Century Journalism: In Great Britain and Ireland* (London: Academia Press, 2009), 3.

[7] Michael Schudson, *Discovering the News* (New York: Basic Books, Inc., Publishers, 1978), 153.

[8] Roger Patching and Martin Hirst, *Journalism Ethics: Arguments and Cases for the Twenty-first Century* (New York: Routledge, 2014), xii. See also: Robert J. Power-Berrey, *The Romance of a Great Newspaper* (London: News of the World, 1932).

surprised to hear that the *News of the World* had been in legal trouble, as legal battles were the newspaper's stock and trade. The frequent threat of legal action against the newspaper was almost a matter of pride in an organization which saw itself as too big to fail and considered civil lawsuits as the cost of doing business. The real problem with the *News of the World* scandal was the criminal charges, in that while people were used to the *News of the World* getting into civil squabbles, criminal charges made the journalism giant look like the arrogant upper crust that the newspaper itself often mocked.[9]

It was also not just that the newspaper had hired private contractors to hack into private cell phones, itself a crime, but it was the reliance on hacking as a journalistic tool that caught the public's attention. Further revelations that public officials were commonly paid to reveal confidential information finally stripped the *News of the World* of all journalistic pretense, and the public began to view it as a criminal organization. There was the suggestion by those involved in the scandal that the people had a right to know, but journalism ethics proved a poor defense, and finally after subpoenas, court appearances, firings and resignations the *News of the World* closed its doors for good on July 10, 2011.[10]

The *News of the World's* closing was yet another symbol of a changing of the guard in journalism, a wearing down of the traditional concept of journalism as a profession on par with traditional professions of doctors, lawyers and the clergy. A criminal enterprise would have been unthinkable among those who had viewed journalism as a profession in previous times as it conflicted with concepts of the adversarial press, the watchdog press and the fourth estate.

## Identifying Journalists

In looking at the need for journalists to be responsible to the public, we seem to understand who the public is, and we recognize responsible journalism, but we are less clear about who the journalists are. A hundred years ago, journalists were easy to identify. The journalists either owned or worked for someone with a printing press, and since there were few printing presses,

---

[9] Lloyd Grove, Mike Giglio, Dan Ephron, and William Underhill, "Rupert's Red Menace," *Newsweek*, July 25, 2011, 40-44.
[10] Alan Rusbridger, "How We Broke the Murdoch Scandal," *Newsweek*, July 25, 2011, 45-47.

journalists were easy to identify.

In the digital world, this question is more complicated, as publication has become ubiquitous, and if we were to label everyone with the capability of publishing a journalist, most individuals in modern times would be called journalists. We can narrow it down, however, by considering bloggers, particularly those who are serious information gatherers, some of who are also full-time journalists. Video blogs on YouTube have become a trend that has made an increasing number of video bloggers wealthy. Many of these individuals comment and report on the news and are considered journalists by themselves and by the public. However, often bloggers and vloggers who talk about the news do not want to be called journalists, even though what they produce falls in that category. For instance, Logan Paul, mentioned earlier in this chapter, has millions of followers but does not call himself a journalist. Likewise, Facebook users who post pictures of public events to Facebook groups may not think of themselves as journalists, even though they are performing a journalistic function of informing the public. The question that must be answered is whether people who do not call themselves journalists but act like journalists are still journalists. Is it possible that they are journalists by default, and therefore de facto journalists? We must ask ourselves whether individuals who produce news should be expected to have journalistic responsibility.

## Journalistic Credibility Today

In modern times specific news outlets have credibility, but many members of the public do not trust the media in general, and there are two possible reasons why. The first reason the public may not trust the media is that it misunderstands what unbiased news is. The public correctly understands the media should publish truth, but sometimes views truth as a report only telling the side of the story that they want to hear, and when this happens, they then consider any unbiased news as negative. In reality, it can happen on both sides of an issue (or more than two sides of an issue), and no topic will be immune from accusations of bias by those who only want to see the presentation of one side. This comes down to the public not understanding and accepting the idea of a marketplace of ideas where information is available, allowing individuals to make their own conclusions. Some individuals use the logic that if ideas they find revolting or dangerous are allowed to spread, the ideas will taint society, and therefore, they see censoring published material as positive societal action.[11] The second reason the public may not trust the news media is that are many people who see journalism as having a responsibility to be unbiased, and when they see news reports that are partisan, they lose faith in journalism.[12] Therefore, journalists who are partisan and journalists who are not partisan both create a belief among citizens that journalism is irresponsible. The first reason is based on an incorrect view of journalism by the public, and the second by an incorrect view of journalism by the journalist.

## The Canons of Journalism: Independence

In the previous chapter we noted that what the Canon of Journalism called independence translates into the journalist being able to write, free from outside influences. This is important in regard to freedom of expression because a voice that is controlled by an outside force cannot be the basis for democracy and an informed electorate. In the rest of this chapter the concept of independence will be examined in the several forms in which it occurs in modern times, and its history in the current state of affairs in the last century. This history is vital to understanding from whence the current legal and ethical views of communication independence emanated. Therefore, this section will describe independence and mitigating factors including partisanship, deregulation, concentration of ownership, the Hutchins Commission, government interference and conflicts of interest.

Partisanship is a challenge to journalistic independence, and in some ways, information in the Digital Age is similar to the Partisan Press Era in that we find many news outlets with one-sided news reports. This may transpire when a journalist focuses just on the facts that are favorable to one perspective or may involve only presenting stories which show one side in a positive light and all other sides in a negative one. Therefore, partisan news goes beyond explaining the facts and presents a one-sided interpretation.[13]

Cable's 24-hour news format is sometimes blamed for the re-emergence of communication partisanship in the twentieth century. Because cable news

---

[11] Joel Feinberg, *The Moral Limits of Criminal Law: Offense to Others* (New York: Oxford University Press, 1985), 79.

[12] Yochai Benkler, Robert Faris and Hal Roberts. *Network News Propaganda: Manipulation, Disinformation, and Radicalization in American Politics* (New York: Oxford University Press, 2018), 377.

[13] Jim A. Kuypers, *Partisan Journalism: A History of Media Bias in the United States* (New York: Rowman & Littlefield, 2013), 147.

organizations have so much time to fill, they have a voracious appetite for programming. Therefore, they are usually set up as discussions, which are financially beneficial to the company. For instance, the time and effort required to put a minute of reporting on the air is much greater than for creating a minute of discussion because dialog requires few resources beyond the host's salary. It has also become popular because of its dramatic and controversial possibilities, the format sometimes being described as producing more heat than light, suggesting programming that provides more sensation than information.[14]

Cable news was the first to expand the area of partisanship in recent times, because cable did not fall under the aegis of the Federal Communications Commission (FCC) and therefore had more freedom. For this reason, they could carry programs that would have been considered too indecent for television.[15] Cable also had an advantage in regard to news, because at one time the FCC had strict rules mandating balancing political coverage on broadcast stations. For example, a radio or television station could lose its license to operate if it could not prove it was providing equal access to political opponents. Broadcasters were even required to contact politicians who had been verbally attacked on air and offer them a chance to respond free of charge, while cable news had no such restrictions.[16]

## Broadcasting Deregulation

In the second half of the twentieth century, broadcasting underwent deregulation as President Ronald Reagan pushed an agenda for less government influence, believing the free market should be allowed to take the place of government regulators such as the FCC. Reagan saw government rules as an attack on the free market which went against his concept of small government. The free market system that Reagan was trying to create was one where supply and demand set the price of market goods, something Scottish Enlightenment writer Adam Smith had referred to as the invisible hand, which was a metaphor for the government having a *laissez-faire*, hands off, approach to business. Ideally, this can occur when there are no monopolies, tariffs or stultifying government guidelines.

---

[14] Markus Prior, *Post Broadcast Democracy: How Media Choice Increases Media Inequality* (New York: Cambridge University Press, 2007), 247.

[15] Jeremy Lipschultz, *Broadcast and Internet Indecency: Defining Free Speech* (New York: Routledge, 2008), 95.

[16] Lesley Hitchens, *Broadcasting Pluralism and Diversity: A Comparative Study of Policy and Regulation* (Portland, OR: Hart Publishing, 2006), 180.

However, some argue that government regulation is needed so that there is an even playing field where the law of supply and demand is not secretly manipulated by powerful individuals, resulting in a government ruled by a wealthy elite, a situation known as an oligarchy.[17]

Deregulation changed the broadcast situation immensely, as deregulation's philosophy was that the market could decide what people wanted on the air. As a result, partisanship increased on broadcast stations as well as cable because it was easier to allow for partisanship than to try to make sure all sides were represented. Partisan discussions were also more dramatic than civil non-biased presentations of all sides and for this reason, partisan news programs could generate higher ratings.[18]

One FCC law called the Fairness Doctrine, which had been created to generate a balanced discussion on broadcast stations, required broadcasters to go to great lengths to achieve equilibrium in covering all sides of an issue. Under the Fairness Doctrine, if an individual presented an issue on a broadcast program it was the broadcasters' responsibility to find representatives of opposing views and give them airtime. If a broadcaster fell short of the Fairness Doctrine, he or she could lose their station license to operate. However, instead of creating more discussion, the Fairness Doctrine did the opposite and actually discouraged it, as broadcasters were avoiding controversy so they would not have to air all sides of an issue.[19] As a result, the Fairness Doctrine was withdrawn in 1987, which allowed partisan topics to be covered without requiring a full airing of alternative views by the opposition. More controversy was aired as a result, but it was not necessarily balanced. Therefore, ending the Fairness Doctrine encouraged partisanship on all sides.[20]

The onset of deregulation also changed the amount of advertising that was allowed on broadcast television. Before deregulation, broadcast stations could only air a certain number of minutes of advertising every hour. After

---

[17] Joseph R. Conlin, *The American Past: A Survey of American History, Volume 2, Since 1865* (Boston: Wadsworth, 2010), 819. See also: Adam Smith, *An Inquiry into the Nature and Causes of the Wealth of Nations* (London: W. Strahan, 1776).

[18] Jennifer Holt, *Empires of Entertainment: Media Industries and the Politics of Deregulation, 1980-1996* (New Brunswick, NJ: Rutgers University Press, 2011), 69.

[19] Steven J. Simmons, *The Fairness Doctrine and the Media* (Berkeley, CA: University of California Press, 1978), 4.

[20] Victor Pickard, *America's Battle for Media Democracy: The Triumph of Corporate Libertarianism and the Future of Media Reform* (New York: Cambridge University Press, 2015), 210.

deregulation, there were no limits and it was said the market would decide what amount of advertising audiences would tolerate. As a result, broadcast stations began to air what was then referred to as program length commercials, which are now called infomercials.[21]

Deregulation also undermined news production. After deregulation, broadcast stations were not pressed as hard to produce programming that was simply good for the public. Since it was believed that the market would decide what programing appealed to audiences, news programming became less of a necessity and more of a luxury. While news programs were maintained because they gave stations and networks prestige, the FCC did not scrutinize programming as carefully.[22]

Another result of deregulation was the removal of a limit as to how many broadcast stations a single entity could own. Before deregulation, there were rules which kept individuals from having a monopoly of broadcast stations. For instance, in the 1970s, broadcast station owners could only own 7 television stations, 7 FM radio stations and 7 AM radio stations. The stations that a network owned outright were called owned and operated stations, while the rest of the stations in a network were independently owned as affiliates and merely contracted to carry the network's programming. The original limit on station ownership was created because it was believed that allowing one individual to own too many stations would give that individual too much power, damaging the plurality of opinions. The conventional wisdom had been that having a multitude of independently owned news sources would provide a check on each other as well as the government.[23]

## Concentration of Ownership

When regulations on the number of stations one person could own were lifted, certain individuals began buying numerous stations to form large conglomerates. Running multi-station operations was cheaper and more financially remunerative for the company owners, even though that action concentrated media power in the hands of a small number of media entrepreneurs and allowed a few individuals to influence news coverage at

---

[21] Dorothy G. Singer and Jerome L. Singer, *Handbook of Children and the Media* (Thousand Oaks, CA: Sage, 2001), 386.
[22] Robert M. Entman, *Democracy without Citizens: Media and Decay of American Politics* (New York: Oxford University Press, 1990), 102.
[23] Norman J. Medoff and Barbara Kaye, *Electronic Media, Then, Now, and Later* (Abingdon, UK: Taylor & Francis, 2013), 50.

many stations, creating media monopolies. Some individuals went from owning 21 radio and television stations in the 1970s to owning thousands today, a situation described as a concentration of ownership. Concentration of ownership occurred directly because of deregulation. Ironically, removing limitations on the number of stations an individual could own defeated the previous mindset that more owners meant numerically more diverse viewpoints.[24]

One of the individuals who took advantage of deregulation was media mogul Rupert Murdoch, the originator of the Fox News channel, a 24-hour news station that began in 1996. From the beginning Fox News was conservatively oriented, with Murdoch hiring longtime Republican media consultant Roger Ailes as its CEO. Ailes had previously advised Republican Presidents Richard Nixon, Ronald Reagan and George Bush, Sr., and was a consultant for Rudy Giuliani's campaign to be mayor of New York City. While Fox was the first overtly partisan news network, it was not the last. However, since the viewing audience for the more liberal oriented news networks was broken up among several options, conservative news viewers tended to stick with Fox News and as a result, it became the single most viewed cable news network for many years.[25]

While CNN founder Ted Turner had started out as a conservative, he turned to liberalism early on. For a time, the two most prominent media moguls were liberal Ted Turner and conservative Rupert Murdoch. Turner hated Murdoch, and verbally attacked him. Some believe the feud started during a yacht race when a boat captained by Turner was run aground by Murdoch's yacht.[26] Turner had been born into money and early on invested in the baseball team the Atlanta Braves as well as Chicago television station WGN, which he eventually parlayed into pioneering the first cable news network (CNN).[27]

---

[24] Robert D. McChesney, *The Problem of the Media: U.S. Communication Politics in the Twenty-First Century* (New York: New York University Press, 2004), 230-1; See also, Ben Bagdikian, *Media Monopoly* (Boston: Beacon Press, 2000).
[25] Kuypers, *Partisan Journalism*, 219-20.
[26] Holt, *Empires of Entertainment Media Industries and the Politics*, 69; Gabriel Sherman, *The Loudest Voice in the Room: How the Brilliant, Bombastic, Roger Ailes Built Fox News and Divided a Country* (New York: Random House Publishing, 2013), 206; Ken Auletta, *Media Man: Ted Turner's Improbable Empire* (New York: W. W. Norton & Company, 2004), 80.
[27] Todd Wilkinson, *Last Stand: Ted Turner's Quest to Save a Troubled Planet* (New York: Rowman & Littlefield, 2013), 62.

On the other hand, Murdoch had started his business in Australia where he was a citizen and later expanded his holdings to tabloids in the United Kingdom. He arrived in the United States as deregulation was occurring but was unable to take advantage of it because he was an Australian citizen, and ownership of broadcasting outlets was limited to those with United States' citizenship. As a result, Murdoch became a U.S. citizen as well as a dual citizen of Australia, allowing him to buy television stations in the United States.[28]

In recent times, just a few powerful companies have gained domination over what individuals see on social media, and much of this is controlled by algorithms. Most people are aware that in search engines, the search results are the product of algorithms coded by the parent company's programmers. This is a threat to information, which is filtered through these computer programs. For instance, it is easy for an algorithm in a search engine or social media program to favor certain biases, which is worrisome if it were to be applied to searches for news or political information, and even more concerning when the artificial intelligence appears to generate racist or sexist results.[29]

Regulation in this area might be sought as an alternative to breaking up the digital monopolies, although that drastic step could be considered as well. While it may seem to be a bridge too far, the alternative is a press controlled by a few individuals who influence what messages are presented to the voting public.[30]

## The Hutchins Commission

After World War II, wealthy owner of *Time* magazine Henry Luce funded a private group to study press responsibility called the Hutchins Commission, and alternately the Commission for a Free and Responsible Press. It was made up of twelve academics who were handpicked by the head of the committee and approved by Luce. Right away the commission

---

[28] Alastair Davison, *From Subject to Citizen: Australian Citizenship in the Twentieth Century* (New York: Cambridge University Press, 1997), 137.

[29] Caitlin Dewy, "Google Maps' White House Glitch, Flickr Auto-Tag, and the Case of the Racist Algorithm," *Washington Post*, May 20, 2015, https://www.washingtonpost.com/news/the-intersect/wp/2015/05/20/google-maps-white-house-glitch-flickr-auto-tag-and-the-case-of-the-racist-algorithm/

[30] Eli M. Noam, *Media Ownership and Concentration in America* (New York: Oxford University Press, 2009), 34.

drew criticism as it seemed impossible that twelve non-journalists could understand what was at stake, and the challenges journalists faced. It also seemed as if the committee had been selected carefully to concoct a predetermined conclusion.[31]

The commission released a report which called for a radical change in communication, suggesting that a new theory should supersede the one which had been in place previously. The previous theory was called the libertarian theory, which gave no restrictions to the press on the basis of the First Amendment. The Hutchins Commission Report was auspiciously called *A Free and Responsible Press* with a title page containing a quote from United States founding father John Adams, which stated: "If there is ever to be an amelioration of the condition of mankind, philosophers, theologians, legislators, politicians and moralists will find that the regulation of the press is the most difficult, dangerous and important problem they have to resolve. Mankind cannot now be governed without, or at present with it."[32]

Despite a title paying homage to the press and the Adams' reference to its importance, the Hutchins Commission advocated for laws to punish journalists who made errors. The greatest concern with the socially responsible viewpoint, however, was that the committee endorsed writing biased stories. The committee did not believe people were capable of taking advantage of the marketplace of ideas, and believed reporters should not only report the facts, but tell people how to think about those facts. They called this moving from an objective model to the interpretive model, which many believed undermined every reason for having the First Amendment. It also upended the concept of unbiased reporting that had developed since the Penny Press.[33]

The departure in what the Hutchins Commission mandated from past ideas was that journalism has a responsibility to the government, not just society,

---

[31] Pickard, *America's Battle for Media Democracy,* 144-6.
[32] Commission on Freedom of the Press, *A Free and Responsible Press: A General Report on Mass Communication: Newspapers, Magazines, Motion Pictures and Books* (Chicago: University of Chicago Press, 1947), title page; The book does not cite the original source, which is the following: John Adams to James Lloyd, February 11, 1815, in *The Works of John Adams*, ed. Charles Francis Adams (Boston: Little, Brown, 1851), vol. 10, 118.
[33] Robert W. McChesney and Victor Pickard, *Will the Last Reporter Please Turn Out the Lights: The Collapse of Journalism and What Can be Done to Fix It* (New York: The New Press, 2011), 178; Commission on Freedom of the Press, *A Free and Responsible Press,* 80.

while the view of the writers of the First Amendment was that the press' responsibility was to be a watchdog over the government, rather than be its employee. The Hutchins Committee even went so far as to say that perhaps the First Amendment guaranteeing freedom of the press should be changed.[34]

These pronouncements from a band of academics did not sit well with First Amendment supporters, and while some liked the idea of putting more context into stories, unbiased reporting continued to be journalism's gold standard. Some scholars, like John Merrill, scoffed at the ideas put forth in the Hutchins Commission, saying it was simply an example of the old style libertarianism with all its old challenges. Merrill was joined in his criticism of the Hutchins Commission by scholars such as Margaret Blanchard and J. Herbert Altschull. Still others like Edward Lambeth in the book *Committed Journalism* emphasized that reporters are part of a public trust and have important responsibilities. Lambeth went even further than the Hutchins Commission had, embracing some classical philosophers and stating that reporters have a duty to do good, which he interpreted to mean being supportive of the government. The social responsibility theory never took root widely in the United States, although it was heavily discussed.[35]

A few years after the Hutchins Commission report was released, several professors wrote a book called *The Four Theories of the Press* about different kinds of governments and how their media operated. It noted that some governments, like the then Soviet Union, ran the media themselves. This book also included one approach which was based on the Hutchins Commission, advocating social responsibility and duty to society.[36]

## Government Regulation

There is a possibility that future regulation could create a digital domain wherein more voices could be heard, with fewer conflicts of interest and if

---

[34] John C. Merrill, *The Imperative of Freedom: A Philosophy of Journalistic Autonomy* (New York: Hastings House Publishers, 1974), 36.

[35] Merrill, *The Imperative of Freedom,* 36; Margaret A. Blanchard, "The Hutchins Commission: The Press and the Responsibility Concept," *Journalism Monographs* 49 (May 1977): 6; Herbert J. Altschull, *Agents of Power* (White Plains, NY: Longman, 1984), 182; Edward Lambeth, *Committed Journalism: An Ethic for the Profession* (Bloomington, IN: Indiana University Press, 1992), 73.

[36] Fred S. Siebert, Theodore Peterson, and Wilber Schramm, *Four Theories of the Press* (Urbana, IL: University of Illinois Press, 1963), 39.

not less biased, at least biased with more transparent sources. However, this troubles some free speech advocates, because government-imposed rules can have unintended consequences. For instance, rules which would require clearly revealed sources of content on the Internet would eliminate some privacy.[37]

Governments throughout history have had a poor record in regard to allowing freedom of speech when it could hurt their interests. Therefore, there is concern that a government's Internet laws could also be implemented in a way that hurts free speech rather than encourages it, as already occurs in some parts of the world such as in China and Russia.[38] Another state which owns a news network is Qatar, which controls the Al-Jazeera network. Al-Jazeera tends to be much more objective than the news within and coming from some other countries, however there have been claims of government bias.[39]

A few democratically run countries also have state run media. Currently, the United States has virtually no state sponsored news with the exception of National Public Radio. However, even NPR is heavily supported by private donations from its listeners, and is editorially independent from the government. Other democratic countries with state run media include Britain and Canada. Britain has the state sponsored British Broadcasting Corporation (BBC), which produces both news and entertainment programming, and has a reputation for being independent from the state. Likewise, Canada has had a long history of funding its radio and television stations, especially with the Canadian Broadcasting Corporation. Not long ago, the Canadian government proposed a system for funding independent news programs in Canada over a five-year period. These would be in the form of grants that would total over half a billion dollars. However, there was concern among journalists that the money might be used to reward news operations favorable to one party or ideology, or to encourage positive reports on those responsible for the funding.[40]

---

[37] Ted Claypoole and Theresa Payton, *Protecting Your Internet Identity: Are You Naked Online?* (Rowman & Littlefield, 2016), 232.

[38] Paul J. Bolt and Sharyl N. Cross, *China, Russia and Twenty-First Century Global Geopolitics* (Oxford, UK: Oxford University Press, 2018), 219.

[39] Hussein Ibish, "Why America Turned Off Al Jazeera," *New York Times*, February 17, 2016, https://www.nytimes.com/2016/02/18/opinion/ why-america-turned-off-al-jazeera.html

[40] Larry Kusch, "Pallister Questions Long-Term Value of Ottawa's Media-Subsidy Plan," *Winnipeg Free Press*, November 23, 2018,

## International Media

While China's low level of speech freedom was broached earlier, its example bears further discussion because of Internet restrictions imposed in the name of national security. Specifically, China's online firewall prevents most interaction between its citizens and the rest of the world. However, there is a new measure that is being rolled out that is further stifling free speech. The system being installed by the Chinese government gives each person in China a social desirability score in reference to how social the government thinks each person is, although it is actually a score based on how compliant a person is to the government. There are many factors that go into the score, but one thing that can give you a bad score is posting news or comments of which the government does not approve, and the retribution can be quite severe. For instance, a low score prevents someone from flying on airplanes or taking long distance trains, which can mean separation from family as well as damaging a person's ability to make a living. With trains being a main form of transportation in China, being banned from them is a severe punishment. In effect, it is a banishment from any place outside of one's immediate town. The Chinese government claims the goal of the punishments is to "bankrupt" individuals with a low social score, and the message from the Chinese government is clear: any attempt to spread a message that disagrees with the party line can lead to financial bankruptcy and social isolation.[41]

This new policy follows another directive which installed hundreds of government workers to monitor postings on China's internal Internet system. This is part of the infrastructure needed to monitor Chinese citizens in order to give them a score telling individuals how much the government likes them or does not like them. There is a further concern for those who are given marginal scores, because if an individual's low score becomes public, others may shy away from contact because of a fear that their own scores will suffer from being associated with a government undesirable.[42]

---

https://www.winnipegfreepress.com/local/pallister-questions-long-term-value-of-ottawas-media-subsidy-plan-501147331.html.

[41] Harry Cockburn, "China Blacklists Millions of People from Booking Flights as Social Credit System Introduced," *Independent*, November 23, 2018, https://www.independent.co.uk/news/world/asia/china-social-credit-system-flight-booking-blacklisted-beijing-points-a8646316.html.

[42] Liu Xuanzun, "Social Credit System Must Bankrupt Discredited People: Former Official," *Global Times*, May 20, 2018,

The impact on what the Chinese are allowed to say on the Internet has to be great, as it is a system designed to stop speech against the government. This is one of the most dangerous ways to prevent free speech in modern times in that the mere threat of punishment will prevent people from saying things that could be interpreted as critical to those in power. This is known as a chilling effect, meaning a bias is created when people are too afraid to talk for fear of reprisals, causing a spiral of silence. While the system is still in the trial stage, punishments have already been given out. According to a Chinese source, by April 2018, China had already blocked 11 million flights and over four million high-speed train trips because of low social scores.[43]

## Conflict of Interest in Relationships

Avoiding conflicts of interest is foundational for journalists. In *Conflicts of Interest in the Professions*, Michael Davis and Andrew Stark noted that "It is precisely because 'the whole truth and nothing but the truth' is unattainable that conflicts of interest pose such a basic threat to the primary interest of journalism."[44]

Sometimes a friendship can be a conflict of interest. An example would be if a journalist's family member was arrested for murder. The journalist might have difficulty in being impartial as natural loyalty to a family member would make it hard for the journalist to write about the situation objectively. This kind of clear-cut example rarely happens, although less obvious journalism friendships often do have conflict of interest possibilities. For example, a potential case of conflict of interest because of a friendship between a reporter and a source occurred at National Public Radio, in which Nina Totenberg was the reporter and the source was Supreme Court judge Antonin Scalia. In the course of her coverage of the court beat, Totenberg had become good friends with Scalia. When some portrayed the judge in an unflattering light, Totenberg came to his defense, describing him in the positive light that she had come to know. This caused Totenberg to be attacked as having a conflict of interest because she was close to her source.[45]

---

http://www.globaltimes.cn/content/1103262.shtml.
[43] Xuanzun, "Social Credit System Must Bankrupt Discredited People," http://www.globaltimes.cn/content/1103262.shtml.
[44] Michael Davis and Andrew Stark, *Conflict of Interest in the Professions* (New York: Oxford University Press, 2001), 78.
[45] Elizabeth Jensen, "When is a Friendship a Conflict of Interest?" *NPR,* February

The Totenberg situation is one that deserved a close look, but not one in which a conflict of interest definitely occurred as the problem of becoming close to sources is an occupational hazard. Because it is considered good journalism to have connections, reporters expend a great deal of effort so that sources will trust them to keep their confidences, and in the course of developing this trust, rapport is cultivated. Consequently, reporters with highly placed friends are valuable because they have access to information not available to the general public. Therefore, the friendship Totenberg had with Scalia could be defended as within the bounds of reasonable and ethical journalism practice.

Since the Penny Press times, reporters have worked on beats, those specific areas where they develop expertise. They also develop friendships in most cases as they often see their sources frequently, sometimes every day. They may learn about their sources' family, friends, likes and dislikes. These friendships, which make it easier to report the news, can also make it difficult to be unbiased, which is why reporters must work hard to keep themselves in balance. In the case of Nina Totenberg, she had reported objectively about Scalia in the past, suggesting that she was telling the truth rather than just showing a bias. The fact that Totenberg had a career's worth of objective reporting also leaned heavily in her favor.[46]

There have been other cases, where there could have been a conflict of interest perception. For instance, when another legendary reporter Andrea Mitchell married Alan Greenspan, the head of the Federal Reserve and a powerful influence on banking, there could have been a conflict of interest. However, Mitchell reported rarely if ever on this area of news and was careful to maintain her objectivity. As a result, her reputation remains impeccable.[47]

Another news presenter found it more difficult to do her job when a family member became part of the news. Les Moonves was CEO of CBS for many years while his wife Julie Chen was a television personality and anchor who obtained a position as on-air talent on CBS's *The Talk*. When allegations were made against Moonves causing him to resign, Chen resigned her

---

26, 2016, https://www.npr.org/sections/ombudsman/2016/02/26/467813499/when-is-a-friendship-a-conflict-of-interest.

[46] Jensen, "When is a Friendship a Conflict of Interest?"

[47] Brian S. Brooks, George Kennedy, Daryl R. Moen, and Don Ranly, *News Reporting and Writing* (Boston: Bedford/St. Martin's, 2011), 477.

position as well, perhaps because the pressure on her to be unbiased about a story involving her husband was too much.[48]

The *New York Times'* rules for reporters discourages them from spending time with sources apart from their work, noting that nothing may be wrong with the relationship, but that it can create an appearance of a conflict of interest. Despite this relationship advice, a 26-year-old *New York Times* reporter who had been nominated for a Pulitzer Prize, had a relationship with a government source. Ali Watkins admitted she had a three-year affair with James Wolfe, whom she had first met as a source. Wolfe was a senior advisor to the United States Senate Intelligence Committee and had a top-secret security clearance. When Wolfe was arrested for lying to investigators about his relationship with Watkins, her emails were seized by federal prosecutors and President Trump tweeted that Wolfe had been leaking information to the *New York Times*. It has not been determined if Wolfe did leak information to Watkins, although the *New York Times* stated it was trying to determine if any of the stories Watkins had written might have been influenced by her relationship. Unlike the preceding examples which contained potentials for a conflict of interest, the *New York Times* case was clearly a conflict of interest that compromised the journalist's integrity.[49]

Sometimes conflict of interest enters by means of newspaper ownership. In the first two and a half centuries of U.S. newspapers, they were almost always owned by an individual with a news or printing background. However, in modern times, that is often not the case with news sources. Most news organizations are owned by larger companies, which can create a concern about conflicts of interest. For instance, a few years ago, Amazon founder Jeff Bezos bought the *Washington Post* for 250 million dollars. However, Bezos told the news staff that he did not expect special treatment, and to do what they felt was journalistically right in their coverage. He promised not to interfere, directly addressing the elephant in the room, that there was a potential conflict of interest. The *Washington Post* journalists were particularly sensitive about this as the newspaper had experienced a

---

[48] Brittany Shoot, "Watch: Julie Chen Quits 'The Talk' Via Video Following the Resignation of Former CBS CEO Les Moonves," *Fortune*, September 18, 2018, http://fortune.com/2018/09/18/watch-julie-chen-quit-the-talk-video-moonves/.

[49] Michael M. Grynbaum, Scotte Shane, and Emily Flitter, "How an Affair Between a Reporter and a Security Aide Has Rattled Washington Media," *New York Times,* June 24, 2018, https://www.nytimes.com/2018/06/24/business/media/james-wolfe-ali-watkins-leaks-reporter.html.

potential conflict of interest with an owner in the past. During the Watergate situation, a Nixon official had threatened reporters by applying pressure on the *Washington Post's* owner Katherine Graham. Bezos referenced the Nixon situation, telling reporters that no one would use him as leverage against a story that the reporters wanted to publish.[50]

## Advertising Conflicts of Interest

Sometimes advertising can create a conflict of interest and can make individuals question a news organization's impartiality. For instance, if a business owner spends a great deal of money to advertise in a newscast, that business owner may feel mistakenly entitled to complimentary coverage by the news department. There have been times when reporters have had stories spiked by a supervisor looking out for the advertising department. Stories that conflict with advertisers can include unfavorable reports about the business or product and/or favorable reports about a rival business. This business influence is less noticeable to the public, as in cases where medical companies sponsor health journalism conventions costing hundreds of thousands of dollars.[51]

Partiality can also come from the corporate level. For instance, Facebook has claimed political neutrality in dealing with news on its platform. However, it has come under fire for attempting to undermine its enemies. One such enemy was billionaire philanthropist George Soros, who makes no secret about legally giving money to the democratic party. However, Soros ran afoul of Facebook when he publicly talked against it at a meeting of elite individuals from around the world. In response, a Facebook official surreptitiously hired a public relations firm to attack Soros, although Facebook founder and CEO Mark Zuckerberg later contended he had no knowledge of this action by his company.[52]

---

[50] David Smith, "Why does Trump Hate Jeff Bezos: Is it About Power or Money?" *The Guardian*, June 17, 2018, https://www.theguardian.com/technology/2018/jun/17/donald-trump-jeff-bezos-amazon-washington-post-power-money.

[51] Gene Foreman, *The Ethical Journalist: Making Responsible Decisions in the Digital Age* (Malden, MA: John Wiley & Sons, Inc., 2015), 377.

[52] Julia Carrie Wong, "Facebook Policy Chief Admits Hiring PR Firm to Attack George Soros," *The Guardian*, November 21, 2018, https://www.theguardian.com/technology/2018/nov/21/facebook-admits-definers-pr-george-soros-critics-sandberg-zuckerberg.

In the almost century since the Canons of Journalism was assembled the elements of responsibility and independence have continued to be factors that information consumers care about and by which message creators are challenged. It appears these elements are enduring values rather than just time-based tribulations of early twentieth century journalists. In the next chapter we examine the canons of sincerity, truthfulness, accuracy and impartiality in light of how they have fared in recent times and in the years since they were listed in the Canons of Journalism.

## Discussion Questions

1. Remember: What changes in the law occurring in the 1980s caused a proliferation of partisanship on broadcast channels?

2. Understand: Deregulation was proposed in order to free up the economic market. What were the side effects to this change in regard to the ability to have unbiased news?

3. Apply: The United States government is looking into regulating social media companies. How is this justifiable or not justifiable in relation to having a free market economic system?

4. Evaluate: How can totally free market forces operate in a system where irresponsible speech is a commercial commodity? Explain how these two aspects of freedom coexist.

5. Create: Assume you are tasked with creating legal guidelines of what is not allowed on social media. Identify three things you would prohibit and justify how denying others the freedom to communicate about these topics would benefit society as a whole.

# CHAPTER SIX

## TODAY'S PROBLEM OF CREDIBILITY PART 2: THE CANONS OF SINCERITY, TRUTHFULNESS, ACCURACY, AND IMPARTIALITY

This chapter continues the scrutiny of ethical elements from the Canons of Journalism in regard to those elements' impact on modern journalism. Whereas Chapter Five examined the Canons of Journalism in respect to responsibility and independence, this chapter focuses on the additional ethical elements of sincerity, truthfulness, accuracy and impartiality. While the Canons of Journalism showed us that these elements were a journalism concern in the early twentieth century, this chapter will visit their status a hundred years hence, to assess whether these elements of the Canons of Journalism represent current challenges.

### The Canons of Journalism: Sincerity, Truthfulness, Accuracy

The Canons of Journalism stated that a truthful account must be complete, an easier task when news was spread by putting ink on paper. In the 1920s when the Canons were written, commercial broadcast radio was only two years old and broadcast news had not been invented. Television did not exist, and the person who would one day invent it was only fifteen years old at the time. Furthermore, in the 1920s, reporters had time to gather information and write reports. Since most newspapers only went to press once a day, reporters had time to get the who, what, when, where and why of a story, double checking the facts before the report went to press and out the door to subscribers.

Almost a century later the situation is very different, as in modern times, reporters have to compete with other media outlets as well as social media such as Twitter. For instance, a citizen journalist may post pictures of an event on Facebook, Twitter, Snapchat or Instagram before the full time journalists in the major media companies are even aware of what has happened. Another reason the situation has changed is the speed of publication. One hundred years ago, a story was often written, typeset, printed and distributed before anyone heard about it, while in the current age information is usually transmitted minutes or even seconds after the news event happens. In the case of live streaming video coverage, the information may be transmitted as it is happening with context coming in piecemeal. While this is a part of our modern culture, this system provides an incomplete picture of news events, as we see the event as it unfolds rather than in a complete form after it is over. Therefore, admonitions from a century ago to write only complete stories may not be as easy to facilitate with today's instant media.

Several recent examples help illustrate this drawback of having news stories trickling in, fact by fact. One illustration of this kind of unfolding story was the California wildfire called Camp Fire. While the audience viewed live video of the fire raging and knew it had swept through the town of Paradise, most of the elements of the story were unknown at first.[1] Another example goes back further in time and is a quintessential live news event. O.J. Simpson's Bronco chase that was broadcast live was a portent of the kind of streaming news that inundates Twitter. It was riveting, but it also carried the problem of a lack of context and the distinct possibility that the chase could end with Simpson's suicide.[2]

Accuracy in journalism is much more difficult to assess than in other fields. For instance, an archer who shoots at a target can calculate accuracy by how close the arrows land in proximity to the target's center and basketball players can evaluate their accuracy by how many basketballs enter the hoop. Each of these can be examined with numbers, and there is little dispute about how close an arrow is to the center of a target, or how many times a basketball went through a hoop. However, trying to gauge how accurate a story is can be much more challenging.

We could start by comparing the account with the actual event and evaluate if the description is different than the actual event. However, this approach assumes we were at the event, and most of the time when we read news

---

[1] Evan Sernoffsky, "Five Firefighters among Dozen-plus Patients Burned in Camp Fire," *San Francisco Chronicle*, November 15, 2018, https://www.sfchronicle.com/california-wildfires/amp/Five-firefighters-among-dozen-plus-patients-13396604.php.
[2] Michael J. Bugeja, *Living Ethics: Developing Values in Mass Communication* (Boston: Allyn & Bacon, 1996), 277, 279.

stories, we are doing it because we want to learn about an occurrence for which we were not present. In the past, news scholars suggested that individuals could tell how accurate a story was by comparing several newspaper accounts. Many individuals used to read multiple newspapers each day, and newspapers were so popular, economy of scale meant they were very cheap. By reading multiple newspapers, people could measure which stories other newspapers were missing, which facts other newspapers had exaggerated, and which newspapers seemed to slant the news one way or the other. This method of looking for accuracy was borrowed from research where it is called triangulation.[3]

Triangulation worked better in the past than it does in modern times, as previous newspapers usually had a staff of reporters which gathered the information themselves and competed against rival newspapers. The news community of even small areas usually consisted of at least one newspaper, one or two television stations and several radio stations. Even small newspapers frequently had a reporter stationed at the state capitol and sometimes one in Washington, D. C. to cover government events affecting their area. Much of the news was home grown, and it was said you could tell how much quality a news operation had by how much of their own news they produced. Even when pressers were given out, reporters still tended to do their own interviews and additional investigation, as writing a story from a media release without extra research was considered lazy reporting. The end result was that for every local story, there were usually a number of reporters covering it. The fact that the Federal Communications Commission (FCC) required radio and television stations to operate in the public interest, further encouraged broadcast stations to cover local events in order to keep their FCC license. As a result, there was an assortment of media voices for comparison. In fact, there were so many journalists at public events that it was sometimes derisively called pack reporting, a phenomenon unambiguously described in the seminal classic *The Boys on the Bus*, which detailed the lives of political reporters on the campaign trail.[4]

The Digital Age changed this situation and the media voices which actually covered events began to disappear at the same time that news sites proliferated on the Internet, providing the appearance of a multiplicity of voices. In reality, while online news sites have flourished, most of these

---

[3] Kim Christian Schroder, "The Best of Both Worlds," in *Rethinking the Media Audience: The New Agenda*, ed. Pertti Alasuutari (Thousand Oaks, CA: Sage, 1999), 50.
[4] Timothy Crouse, *The Boys on the Bus* (New York: Random House, 2003).

recycle news from other sites, and the actual reporter who witnesses events firsthand are much rarer. Martin Conboy in *Journalism Studies* noted: "Studies of journalists in news media organizations demonstrate unequivocally that technology has been used as a way of increasing productivity and output with fewer journalists doing more writing based on less and less primary research."[5]

International news also once had many more voices representing it. For example, there were a number of news wire services that carried overseas news and had reporters stationed in exotic ports of call. United Press International (UPI) and the Associated Press (AP) were two of the most popular wire services used by television, radio and newspapers, while others included *Havas* and *Agence France Presse*.[6]

When the Internet became popular, it, rather than radio and television stations, became the public's main news source. Satellite radio also increased competition, causing many radio stations to go out of business. This was a time when the FCC began to be less strict in enforcing community involvement among radio stations because of deregulation, which meant broadcast news operations were no longer required to demonstrate that a station was operating in the public interest. Another aspect of deregulation that hurt radio was the ability of a single entity to own unlimited stations, a phenomenon which resulted in media concentration of ownership, a topic touched on in the previous chapter. This meant there were still many stations, but only a few individuals controlling them. Additionally, because local programming including news was more expensive to run than simply airing a national feed, owners often standardized the radio stations, offering national programming and eliminating local inputs.[7]

The shrinking number of radio stations hurt the overall production of news because the local radio stations were the ones who fed news to UPI and AP. Local stations who were associated with the AP fed stories to their headquarters as members of a news cooperative. Alternately, all radio stations could feed stories to the UPI as paid stringers. When local news

---

[5] Martin Conboy, *Journalism Studies: The Basics* (New York: Routledge, 2013), 159.
[6] David T. Z. Mindich, *The Mediated World: A New Approach to Mass Communication and Culture* (Lanham, MD: Rowman and Littlefield, 2019), 397; Kent Cooper, *Barriers Down: The Story of the News Agency Epoch* (Port Washington, NY: Kennikat Press, 1942), 7.
[7] C. Edwin Baker, *Media Concentration and Democracy: Why Ownership Matters* (New York: Cambridge University Press, 2006), 126.

people lost jobs because of the shrinking news force, the local voices where the wire services obtained news disappeared. International news also suffered from shrinking staffs. At one time major networks and newspapers had news bureaus in major and even minor cities throughout the world, along with ample budgets. The reporters in each country knew the culture and the people and could report stories accurately when they happened. The news organizations felt they had to do this, because they were afraid to be the only ones not adequately reporting from a country when a story broke.[8]

The television networks poured a great deal of money into their news divisions, because a network's news operation was considered a showcase of the network's quality. Today, network television news still commands respect, but the amount of credibility and the resources given to it are a fraction of what it was a few decades ago. The vanishing resources given to news operations means that there are fewer individuals digging for stories. It has also affected how news is gathered, and both of these factors have had an impact on accuracy. In previous times, reporters often met sources in person to do interviews, where reporters asked questions and tried to see if they could access the source's credibility and watch for holes in the source's story. This approach facilitated the uncovering of unscrupulous individuals who fabricated information. Usually publishing the source's own response to pointed questions revealed a great deal, as a short quote, soundbite or video clip can expose the truth. Though the news interview is much rarer in modern times, it had been a standard since the days of the Penny Press.[9]

In modern times, the digital distribution system and physically distant information gathering method favors the source rather than the public, positioning journalism at a disadvantage from the inception. Additionally, journalists are given the job of producing many stories in a short period of time. News organization owners favor this system, because they receive content per reporter with quality and accuracy as the only casualties. Often, the reporters are put in the awkward situation of having to generate stories directly from the Internet. Therefore, instead of going to an event, they may pull pictures and comments from social media, where tweets replace interviews, and in many cases, reporters email or text questions to sources.

---

[8] Garrick Utley, *Live from the Trenches: The Changing Role of Television News* (Carbondale, IL: University of Southern Illinois Press, 1998), 84.
[9] George H. Douglas *The Golden Age of Newspapers* (Westport, CT: Greenwood Press, 1999), 33.

None of this allows the reporter to probe for accuracy, which can take a back seat to producing content.[10]

Turning to the Internet for stories can create other problems as well. A number of years ago the author was in a situation in which many news outlets were wiped out by a natural disaster in a U.S. city (New Orleans after Hurricane Katrina). Residents in the area availed themselves of an Internet bulletin board to report information, and from the reports, it appeared that there were riots throughout New Orleans, as many different witnesses posted about hearing shots being fired. Later, it was clear there had not been widespread rioting, although the residents' reporting of the gun shots was accurate. However, in putting all the reports together from the bulletin board, the public concluded that there were many widespread incidents. In fact, unknown to the people who reported hearing the gun shots, whom all lived in the same neighborhood, they were describing a single situation. Rather than a crimewave the group had concluded was occurring, a single man had been firing a gun into the air. This is the kind of problem that occurs when there are no reporters to verify the information, and why simply getting information from anonymous citizen journalists can lead to inaccuracies.

## Journalism by Non-Journalists

Several decades ago, there was great hope in the idea that technology would allow the public to record and report what they witnessed, increasing the amount of accurate news coverage. This was called citizen journalism, and with it came the expectation of inexhaustible transparency, which occasionally occurred. In certain cases, where public servants have failed to live up to their responsibilities, privately recorded video by citizen journalists subsequently made public has shown that standards were not being met, and in some cases criminal acts had occurred. Despite the good that this has brought about in some cases, citizen journalists are not trained to prevent bias and may have an agenda, provoking skepticism. Additionally, citizen journalists may take a situation out of context and may make poor journalistic decisions.[11]

---

[10] Rena Bivens, *Digital Currents: How Technology and the Public are Shaping News* (Toronto, Canada: University of Toronto Press, 2014), 167.

[11] Stephen Quinn and Stephen Lamble, *Online Newsgathering: Research and Reporting for Journalism* (Burlington, MA: Focal Press, 2012), 55.

The difficulty with citizen journalism news is that much of what individuals on the Internet find, whether it is on Twitter, Facebook or Instagram, is rumors. Often the discussion is what might be true, based on speculation. Usually the conversations start with facts, but when no new facts emerge, the discussion becomes more and more speculative, because sensational rumors are often more interesting than the truth.[12]

Because of the anonymity of the Internet, citizen journalism is a journalistic risk because the unidentified Internet user has no trepidation of punishment for lying. Therefore, citizen journalism can reveal what individuals are saying about something, but it does not show if it is true, and reporting rumors on the Internet can give traction to stories that are false. Because of the problems of anonymity, some online news sources do not even allow anonymous statements in their comments section and require commenters to open an account first. While this can give the news organization the commenter's server Internet provider information, it still does not give them the commenter's identity and the reader does not know if the commenter is a legitimate responder, or a paid product representative.

Another aspect of citizen journalism is a phenomenon called ambient news, which refers to the fact that news is everywhere on the Internet and is constantly being created by both professional and non-professional sources. This ambiguousness of sourcing adds to the challenge of assessing Internet news' level of truth.[13] Journalism authors Stephen Quinn and Stephen Lamble have noted that audience generated news can lead to legal challenges for a news outlet, and to insure against these have developed three processes: review all audience generated content before publication, trust the citizen journalists or use a computer program to search for key words that indicate a problem. The authors noted that none of these are efficient or necessarily effective.[14]

Some journalists have used an evolved form of citizen journalism called crowdsourcing, which exploits the Internet's human resources to produce a story. One beneficial example of crowdsourcing journalism pertaining to a

---

[12] Martin Hirst, *Navigating Social Journalism: A Handbook for Media Literacy and Citizen Journalism* (New York: Routledge, 2019), 127-8, 133-5.

[13] Zizi Papacharissi, *Affective Publics: Sentiment, Technology, and Politics* (New York, Oxford University Press, 2015), 46, 47; Hirst, *Navigating Social Journalism*, 128. See also the researcher who coined the term "ambient news" at the following: Alfred Hermida, "Twittering the News: The Emergence of Ambient Journalism," *Journalism Practice* 4, no. 3 (July 2010): 297-308.

[14] Quinn and Lamble, *Online Newsgathering*, 54.

database occurred with the *Guardian* newspaper in 2009, when the *Guardian* requested the public's help in reviewing open source documents relating to public officials because it was too large a job for the newspaper to achieve alone. The response was great, and the *Guardian* uncovered major wrongdoing, as in excess of 27,000 readers reviewed over half a million pages of documents, leading to actual arrests of public workers. The advantage of the *Guardian's* approach was that they could double check all the findings that were submitted to them, so they did not rely on the trustworthiness of the public volunteers alone.[15]

In the above example, the *Guardian* side-stepped a major problem with crowdsourcing, which is anonymity of sources. The Internet has introduced an anonymous quality to speech that is unmatched in history. In the past, speech was easily traced to its source and print could be traced to an individual printing press. Today it is easy to be anonymous on the Internet simply by obtaining an email account. While law enforcement can track emails with the help of the account providers and through Internet provider (IP) numbers, journalists do not have that capability. The reason Russian hackers were able to spread information was by using the anonymity of Facebook, which had requirements that could be circumvented.[16] While these kind of threats to certain journalism projects exist, researchers have still suggested that the proper protocols can create credible crowdsourcing.[17]

Another threat to accuracy is framing, which is how a story is presented. Framing focuses on what facts individuals choose to tell a narrative and how they present it. A report can be told in a way that favors an individual but can also be told in a manner which makes that individual appear as a villain.[18] Framing was first discovered by psychologists who established that individuals' real life situations did not always reveal whether they would be happy or sad. For instance, one individual might look at a job promotion as an advantageous opportunity, while another individual might

---

[15] Jim Foust, *Online Journalism: Principles and Practices of News on the Web,* 3rd ed. (New York: Routledge, 2017).

[16] Scott Shane, "The Fake Americans Russia Created to Influence the Election," *New York Times*, September 7, 2017, https://www.nytimes.com/2017/09/07/us/politics/russia-facebook-twitter-election.html.

[17] Tanja Aitamurto, "Crowdsourcing in Open Journalism: Benefits, Challenges, and Value Creation," in *The Routledge Companion to Digital Journalism Studies*, eds. Bob Franklin and Scott A. Eldridge III (New York: Routledge, 2018), 192.

[18] Robert M. Entman, "Framing: Toward Clarification of a Fractured Paradigm," *Journal of Communication* 43, no. 4 (Autumn 1993), 51-58.

find the same job promotion to be an unpleasant stress, fearing that he or she will not have the talent to excel in the new position. Each of these individuals frames the situation differently, and while the facts are the same, the viewpoints are distinctly dissimilar. Psychologists concluded that interpretation was what determined attitude, and the interpretation was based on whether the person framed a situation positively or negatively. This kind of framing in psychology is called a cognitive bias.[19]

It was later discovered that reporters also had frames, in that they could use the manner of presentation to present a politician as a strong leader, or as a threat to the public. In both cases, the narratives might be based on facts, although the frames determined which facts were presented. The framing might be intentional or unintentional, but it creates a concern that partisan reporters could generate stories framing the facts to support a political position. Audiences who agree with the partisan position may not notice the framing, but audiences who are in an opposing position will often recognize it, even if they do not know what it is called.[20]

## Fabrication

Fabrication is concerned with a reporter making up non-fact-based stories, which is an extreme case of inaccuracy and is associated with hoaxes where the entire story is made up, something that occurs in fringe and conspiracy news organizations. There are very few cases in the last fifty years where reputable news sources have been found to have fabricated a report. However, in most where it was discovered, the reporters were punished for their bad behavior. Thom Loeb, in *Editing for the Digital Age* notes: "This is a slam dunk: no journalist should ever do it. As we see when we look at ethics codes, the fundamental rule of journalism should be to tell the truth."[21]

Newspaper fabrications are not new. In fact, the most famous historic fabrication took place in 1835 England, in a newspaper called *The Sun,* which carried six articles apparently detailing the work of an astronomer

---

[19] Amos Tversky and Daniel Kahneman, "Judgment Under Uncertainty, Heuristics and Biases," *Science* 185, no. 4157 (September 1974), 1124. This is a foundational source for prospect theory.
[20] Erving Goffman, *Frame Analysis: An Essay on the Organization of Experience* (New York: Harper & Row, 1974), 10, 11.
[21] Thom Loeb, *Editing for the Digital Age* (Thousand Oaks, CA: CQ Press 2016), 104.

and his surprising discoveries about the moon, a story mentioned briefly in an earlier chapter. The astronomer was well known, but the report about him was completely false. It claimed that the astronomer had used an amazing new telescope to view the moon and that there were animals there including unicorns and humans who flew around like bats. This was all supposedly related to the reporter by a scientist named Grant who was also fictional. After stringing the audience along, the series came to an end without the writer ever admitting it was a hoax. The imaginary scientist Grant claimed the sun's rays had come through the telescope and set fire to a laboratory on the Cape of Good Hope. The author later admitted to writing the story, which may have been plagiarized from author Edgar Allen Poe. The newspaper series author's motive is not known, although it could have been financial. This tall tale is historically known as the Moon Hoax. News hoaxes in recent times have caused a great deal of concern, as fabrications undermine individual's confidence in news, and the effectiveness of a democracy.[22]

Another of the most famous of the news fabrications occurred with a reporter named Janet Cooke who worked for the *Washington Post*, where she wrote a story about an alleged eight-year old heroin addict in the inner city of Washington, D.C. It was well written, tugged at reader's heart strings and contained what seemed like authentic quotes.[23]

Cooke's resume contended she had a master's degree from Vassar. It seemed this young reporter was destined to be a superstar, and soon she was, when her story was submitted to the Pulitzer Prize committee and won. The story, called "Jimmy's World," immediately gained attention, including from the mayor of Washington, D. C., where Jimmy supposedly lived. Soon people all over the city were looking for the little boy, to no avail. It was at this point that some individuals, from city officials to other reporters questioned whether the story was true. The *Washington Post* investigated further and finally Cooke confessed to making the story up, at which point she returned the Pulitzer Prize. It was also discovered that she had never had a degree from Vassar, could not speak several languages and could not play the piano as she had claimed.[24]

---

[22] Matthew Goodman, *The Sun and the Moon* (New York: Basic Books, 2008), 147.
[23] Warren G. Bovee, *Discovering Journalism* (Westport, CT: Greenwood Press, 1999), 101.
[24] Philip Nobile, "The Pulitzer Surprise: The Washington Post's 'Jimmygate,'" *New York Magazine*, April 27, 2020.

One of the parts of "Jimmy's World" that the public had difficulty believing was how easily the other *Washington Post* reporters had been hoodwinked. In fact, the editor who nominated "Jimmy's World" for the Pulitzer was Bob Woodward, who had been instrumental in exposing the Watergate break-in, and the *Washington Post* executive editor at the time was renowned journalist Ben Bradlee.[25]

Another problem with fabrication involved news anchor and managing editor of the *NBC Nightly News* Brian Williams. In addition to his news anchor responsibilities, Williams also became a minor celebrity, appearing on non-news programs including Jon Stewart's *The Daily Show*. After his appearance on *The Daily Show*, Williams was called to task because of a spectacular story he divulged about a helicopter ride in Iraq, that was originally said to have involved enemy missiles and small arms fire. However, Williams' retelling of the event did not match what others said actually happened, and Williams was accused of making up parts of the story to make it more sensational. As a result, he was suspended for six months. Williams apologized publicly for misrepresenting the story, and he returned to NBC in 2015 after the suspension.[26]

The labeling of stories as fake news has become popular among politicians whenever a story arises that attacks their positions, a trend encouraged by President Donald Trump. Actually, much of this politically unpleasant news has been the legitimate practice of adversarial journalism, which involves journalists keeping watch over the government as the Fourth Estate. While Trump's claim that he is frequently attacked by a skeptical media is undeniable, it is not the same as fake news, in that journalist aggressiveness cannot be equated with fabrication.[27]

Trump is not alone in not appreciating an adversarial press, as every United States president has had disagreements with journalists. For instance, the

---

[25] Ben Bradlee, *The Good Life: Newspapering and Other Adventures* (New York: Simon Schuster, 2017).

[26] Susan Keith, "Scandal at the Top in TV News," in *Scandal in a Digital Age*, ed. Hinda Mandell and Gina Masullo Chen (New York: Palgrave Macmillan, 2016), 161.

[27] Marvin Kalb, *The Enemy of the People: Trump's War on the Press, The New McCarthyism, and the Threat to American Democracy* (Washington, DC: The Brookings Institution, 2018), 2; Jesus Velasco, *American Presidential Elections in a Comparative Perspective: The World is Watching* (Lanham, MD: Rowman and Littlefield, 2019), 14. See also: Jim Acosta, *The Enemy of the People: A Dangerous Time to Tell the Truth in America* (New York: Harper, 2019).

public seems to forget that the president who was once labeled the great communicator had a rocky relationship with the media. President Ronald Reagan and later President George Bush, Sr. grudgingly respected rude and annoying reporters such as Sam Donaldson. In fact, during Reagan's later years in office, pressers, or press conferences as they were called, in the Whitehouse almost ceased to exist. The only time reporters actually saw Reagan was when he would walk from the White House to his waiting helicopter, and during those times he would usually motion that he could not hear the journalists' shouted questions over the roar of Air Force One's rotors.[28]

The public additionally seems to forget the history which tells us that one president who won by a landslide and later fell, had a strong dislike, perhaps even hatred, for the press. President Richard Nixon was highly antagonistic to the media long before he became president.[29] Trump is also not the first president to ban a reporter from the White House, as popular columnist George Will was banned from the White House during George Bush Senior's time there, because Will had called the Bush a lapdog. In all these cases, however, journalists were being adversarial, which is what being a watchdog dictates.[30]

Advancements in the Digital Age are also helping fabrications. New technology, as easy to use as a computer app, can simulate a video likeness or a voice in ways that have not been possible before. Some of these simulations have been released as jokes and have been taken seriously, such as a video which seemed to show Trump making negative statements about Belgium politics. After the video surfaced, it was subsequently circulated as real in Europe. However, the video had been produced as a joke using software with special algorithms that took existing parts of Trump's communication and created simulated speech that was almost indistinguishable from Trump's. Some Europeans thought it was real and reacted negatively to it. However, when the creator was tracked down, he

---

[28] Michael Schudson, *The Power of News* (Cambridge, MA: Harvard University Press, 1995), 130; Sam Donaldson, *Hold On, Mr. President* (New York: Fawcett Crest, 1987), 290.
[29] Louis Leibovich, *Richard Nixon, Watergate and the Press: A Historical Perspective* (Westport, CT: Greenwood Publishing Group, 2003), 27.
[30] George Will, "George Bush: The Sound of a Lapdog," *Washington Post*, Jan. 30, 1986.

admitted it had been made as a joke, with no intention of it being taken seriously. These videos have become known as deep fakes.[31]

Another deep fake video hoax that made the rounds on Facebook, was of a large airplane that did a complete 360-degree roll before landing. Except for the fact that based on the laws of physics, large airplanes cannot recover from an upside-down position, the video looked credible, and the video clip was labeled as a news story. However, it turned out to be nothing more than a digital manipulation by a Hollywood animator who had put the clip onto YouTube as an example of his character generated work.[32]

Still another doctored video with real implications was aired at a media conference by White House spokesperson Sarah Sanders. The video showed a White House reporter giving what looked like a karate chop to the arm of a White House assistant. It turned out the video had been sped up so that the reporter's arm appeared to move much faster than it actually had. While the White House did not create the video, it was guilty of publishing it and claiming it was real.[33]

## The Canons of Journalism: Impartiality

In regard to impartiality, some people question whether it continues to have a place in modern journalism. However, recent studies indicate much of the public still wants objective journalism.[34] From a communication perspective, if journalists believe the traditional view that journalism should help

---

[31] Oscar Schwartz, "You Thought Fake News Was Bad? Deep Fakes Are Where Truth Goes to Die," *The Guardian*, November 12, 2018, https://www.theguardian.com/technology/2018/nov/12/deep-fakes-fake-news-truth.

[32] Geoffrey A. Fowler, "I Fell for Facebook Fake News. Here's Why Millions of You Did, Too," *The Washington Post,* October 18, 2018, https://www.washingtonpost.com/technology/2018/10/18/i-fell-facebook-fake-news-heres-why-millions-you-did-too/?utm_term=.bd3e078762a1.

[33] Paul Farhi, "Sarah Sanders Promotes an Altered Video of CNN Reporter, Sparking Allegations of Visual Propaganda," *Washington Post,* November 8, 2018, https://www.washingtonpost.com/lifestyle/style/sarah-sanders-promotes-an-altered-video-of-cnn-reporter-sparking-allegations-of-visual-propaganda/2018/11/08/33210126-e375-11e8-b759-3d88a5ce9e19_story.html?utm_term=.5c51bf3a8412.

[34] Richard Sambrook, "Objectivity and Impartiality in Digital News Coverage," *The Guardian*, June 12, 2014, https://www.theguardian.com/media/media-blog/2014/jun/12/objectivity-and-impartiality-in-digital-news-coverage.

society, the communitarian view, then those involved in making news need to assure the public that it is impartial.[35]

One problem with the Internet is that it is challenging to separate fact from opinion, and both of those from outright untruths. This goes back to the problem discussed earlier regarding anonymity which protects those who tell untruths on the Internet. The anonymity of the Internet allows an individual to claim to be publishing facts, while they are in fact dissembling. Therefore, the real difference in the partisan press from two hundred years ago and the one we have, is that in centuries past, the presses were known, and the printers were accountable. The problem in modern times is that we do not always know what is real and who is providing information, which would provide clues as to whether a story was impartially written. There have been indications that the United States' government is interested in making changes in regard to false stories on the Internet, and has focused attention on the owners of Google, Facebook and Twitter. However, there is no sign of major change, other than the promises of the social media giants that they are trustworthy.[36]

More than ever, information on the Internet needs to be transparent, but the anonymity of the Internet prevents this by concealing fabrication perpetrators and their motives. If information is being published by an advocate, that partiality should be made known. If an individual is getting paid by a sponsor, that person's payment needs to be divulged. In short, revealing this information would reduce the violator's credibility, as it should. Only truly impartial information should have the privilege of being presented as unbiased. Furthermore, in regard to traditional news organizations, reporters should not be in the opinion business, because at the point a reporter is giving opinions, they have become a commentator. While not everything needs to be impartial, news consumers need to have a way to tell which is which. When an anonymous individual pretends to be impartial and is not, he or she is defrauding the audience, something that

---

[35] Hanno Hardt, "Reinventing the Press in the Age of Commercial Appeals: Writings on and about Public Journalism," in *The Idea of Public Journalism,* ed. Theodore Lewis Glasser (New York: Guilford Press, 1999), 205.
[36] Cecilia Kang, David Streitfeld, and Annie Karni, "Antitrust Troubles Snowball for Tech Giants as Lawmakers Join In," *New York Times*, June 3, 2019, https://www.nytimes.com/2019/06/03/technology/facerowmanbook-ftc-antitrust.html

remains true whether the communicator is a journalist or a citizen.[37]

## False Balance Versus the Whole Truth

One aspect of impartiality is trying to maintain a balance between competing viewpoints. For instance, if two candidates are running in an election, the traditional view is to give equal time, emphasis and treatment to both of them, an idea based on the marketplace of ideas. If one candidate is truthful and the other not, presenting both candidates to the public will allow voters to decide who is telling the truth. It might seem easier for reporters to simply inform the public of who is telling the truth and for whom they should vote, a position advocated by the Hutchins Commission discussed in the previous chapter. However, if reporters simply gave their opinion, they would be commentators not journalists, as the journalist's job is not telling individulas what to think but giving them the information that they need to decide what to think.

Some journalists have questioned whether they should skip the step of letting the people decide. This new attack on impartial journalism is called false balance. The rational is that if there are two sides of an issue and the reporter believes one side is true, he or she should not present the ideas equally, but provide information suggesting one or the other is better. This, however, makes the reporter a gatekeeper, and is the opposite of objectivity. Rather than providing a marketplace of ideas, these journalists present a clear indication of what the public is expected to think.[38]

## Discussion Questions

1. Remember: What were the elements discussed in this chapter from the Canons of Journalism? Describe what each of them is in regard to journalism.

2. Understand: How can citizen journalism, crowdsourced journalism, Internet anonymity and framing work against good journalism?

---

[37] Jim A. Kuypers, *Partisan Journalism: A History of Media Bias in the United States* (Lanham, MD: Rowman & Littlefield, 2013), 55.
[38] Mitchell Stephens, *Beyond the News: The Future of Journalism* (New York: Columbia University Press, 2014), 121.

3. Apply: Can the factors described in the above question work in favor of journalism as well? If any or all can be useful to journalism, describe how and defend their use.

4. Evaluate: In regard to false balance, some reporters believe views that they feel are false should not be represented. How many reasons can you provide to defend the idea that all sides of a story should be given, even if some are improbable?

5. Create: The section on made up stories gives many examples. Can you come up with three guidelines that would help you recognize falsehoods in these kinds of news reports?

# CHAPTER SEVEN

# TODAY'S PROBLEM OF CREDIBILITY PART 3: THE CANONS OF FAIR PLAY AND DECENCY

This chapter continues the theme of the last two chapters in looking at the modern problem of credibility through the lens of the Canons of Journalism's last two elements, fair play and decency, covering the areas of privacy, gatekeeping and sensationalism. In Chapter Four we observed how they affected journalists at the canons' inception, and now we look at whether they are still applicable today.

## The Canons of Journalism: Fair Play

Regarding fair play, the canons explain that "A newspaper should not publish unofficial charges affecting reputation or moral character without opportunity given to the accused to be heard; right practice demands the giving of such opportunity in all cases of serious accusation outside judicial proceedings."[1] The explanation adds that what the public is curious about, is not necessarily the same thing as what they have the right to know. This rule of ethics called fair play in the canons, therefore, focuses on privacy, a factor of legal and ethical importance.[2]

Privacy in published communication has been a concern as long as individuals have been talking about free speech. For instance, when John Milton wrote *Areopagitica* he addressed the problem of leaders claiming they had a right not to have their bad acts exposed. Milton wrote that good leaders did not need to worry about having their deeds known to the world, claiming only bad leaders were afraid of the truth. *Cato's Letters* echoed this idea.[3]

---

[1] Paul Alfred Pratte, *Gods Within the Machine: A History of the American Society of Newspaper Editors, 1923-1993* (Westport, CT: Praeger, 1995), 205-6.
[2] Pratte, *Gods Within the Machine, 206.*
[3] John Milton, *Areopagitica: A Speech of Mr. John Milton for the Liberty of Unlicenc'd Printing, to the Parliament of England* (London: n. p., 1644), 40.

The right to privacy is a direct challenge to the right of freedom of speech, a condition scholars call competing rights, suggesting a balance is needed among them. Samuel Warren and Louis Brandeis wrote an important essay about the right to privacy in 1890, and it became a cornerstone for discussions on the topic since.[4] The essay reflected on the law and held that while there was a right to privacy the laws at the time did not protect it. Subsequently, jurists have tried to further determine what the right to privacy means, and how it can be protected, such as in 1965 when Justice Hugo Black lamented that there was not a specific discussion of a privacy right in the Constitution.[5] However, while the Constitution does not explicitly guarantee a right of privacy, the United States Supreme Court has said several amendments in the Bill of Rights implicitly assure it.[6]

The right to privacy concept in present times is being rethought in the light of the contemporary culture of ubiquitous personal transparency, in that many individuals freely divulge personal information on social media, a situation sometimes called oversharing. For instance, an individual may post a video on Facebook of themselves making breakfast, post a picture on Instagram of lunch and tweet the contents of dinner in the evening, before going on a drive that is live streamed on YouTube. Therefore, while the individuals' homes are still their castles, the castle walls are increasingly translucent.[7]

Privacy is becoming a more complicated concept in that although an individual's neighbors may not know what those living next to them are buying on Amazon, computer cookie reading marketing corporations do know, and are quick to offer related products. Similarly, pictures designed to be private, may be posted by someone bent on revenge. Furthermore, in the United States individuals may face online attacks which contain false statements, yet find the material difficult to purge, because of the argument that it is free speech. Conversely, in Europe this is not the case since a passing of the law called the European General Data Protection Regulation,

---

[4] Samuel Warren and Louis Brandeis, "The Right to Privacy," *Harvard Law Review* 193, no. 4, December 15, 1890, 193-220.
[5] Leonard Levy, *Origins of the Bill of Rights* (New Haven, CT: Yale University Press, 2001), 243.
[6] Joe Mathewson, *Law and Ethics for Today's Journalist* (New York: Routledge, 2015), 59; Andrew McStay, *Privacy and the Media* (Los Angeles: Sage Publications, 2017), 28.
[7] Ben Agger, *Oversharing: Presentations of Self in the Internet Age* (New York: Routledge, 2015), 2.

which is based on the idea that an individual being in public does not mean that person relinquishes all privacy rights.[8] In other ways, individuals sometimes misunderstand their right to privacy in public as well, in that some members of the public may think that a photographer must have permission in order to photograph them in public, but this is not a legal right in the United States.[9]

The challenge is usually not whether pictures can be taken in public, but whether the pictures or videos taken in public can be published. Usually they can. However, if a picture depicts someone in a false light and it is published, the injured party can sue, and possibly win. This is the difference between taking a picture and publishing a picture. For example, Google Maps is free to video almost anything visible from a satellite or the street in the United States. However, when it publishes material, it pixilates faces and license plates to ease privacy concerns.[10]

One area of false light that has not been a problem in the past but is today is that of mislabeled pictures, a phenomenon now quite common in picture sharing cites where mislabeling a picture and putting a different slant on the actual context can create a humorous composite. Sometimes these are put into meme formats and widely shared. In some cases, the pictures are of public figures who are accustomed to being in the public eye, while in other cases, where private people have become the subject of memes, the normally unknown have celebrated their new-found fame. However, one can legally invade privacy when using someone's picture without their knowledge. If the picture represents them in a false light, however, it crosses a legal line, and if the person loses a job, or a job opportunity because of it, there can be grounds for a successful lawsuit against the creator.[11]

---

[8] Kristie Byrum, *The European Right to be Forgotten: The First Amendment Enemy* (New York: Lexington Books, 2018), xiii; Adam D. Moore, *Privacy Rights: Moral and Legal Foundations* (University Park, PA: Penn State Press, 2010), 87.

[9] Claude Hubert Cookman, *American Photojournalism: Motivations and Meanings* (Evanston, IL: Northwestern University Press, 2009), 198.

[10] Kush Wadhwa and Rowena Rodrigues, "Evaluating Privacy Impact Assessments," in *Privacy and Security in the Digital Age: Privacy in the Age of Super-Technologies*, ed. Michael Friedewald and Ronald J. Pohoryles (New York: Routledge, 2016), 174.

[11] Jasmine Garsd, "Internet Memes and 'The Right to be Forgotten,'" *NPR*, March 3, 2015, https://www.npr.org/sections/alltechconsidered/2015/03/03/390463119/internet-memes-and-the-right-to-be-forgotten.

This dilemma of privacy versus free speech has been handled differently in different countries. For instance, Europe has much stronger Internet privacy laws than the United States. Specifically, Europe has a right to be forgotten concept that includes the right of an individual to remove information from the Internet. Europe's stronger privacy laws may stem from cultural differences between Europe and the United States, or the fact that most major Internet companies are based in the United States and have lobbying power with United States' lawmakers.[12]

One of the principles behind the Constitution is that government needs to be monitored closely by society, which is the reason the First Amendment allows for freedom of the press. The creators of the Constitution believed that, left to themselves, most leaders would not necessarily do the right thing, and framers had experience with ruthless English royalty to back up their belief. For this reason, government leaders have been seen as having less of a right to privacy than normal citizens in a democracy.[13]

This means that something could be legally published about an elected official, that might not be legal to publish about an individual who has not chosen to be a public person. Therefore, the right to privacy is generally more limited for people who are in the public eye, because if an individual thrusts himself or herself into the spotlight, the individual usually loses status as a private citizen, a condition true for candidates of public office as well as the office holders themselves.[14]

The lower standard of privacy for public officials often extends to celebrities as well. The law looks at the fact that celebrities have voluntarily tried to gain public attention as evidence that they are public figures. Still, even stories about public individuals must be true, as illustrated in the following cases. In a famous case regarding the *National Enquirer*, celebrity Carol Burnett sued and won. The case resulted from a published report saying that Burnett had been publicly drunk, when in fact she had not. In

---

[12] Eric Posner, "We All Have the Right to be Forgotten," *Slate*, May 14, 2014, https://slate.com/news-and-politics/2014/05/the-european-right-to-be-forgotten-is-just-what-the-internet-needs.html; See also: Meg Leta Jones, *Ctrl + Z: The Right to be Forgotten* (New York: New York University Press, 2018); George Brock, *The Right to be Forgotten: Privacy and the Media in the Digital Age* (New York: I. B. Taurus & Co., 2016).

[13] Vikram Amar, *The First Amendment, Freedom of Speech: Its Constitutional History and Contemporary Debate* (Amherst, NY: Prometheus Books, 2009), 87.

[14] Ovadia Ezra, *Moral Dilemmas in Real Life: Current Issues in Applied Ethics* (Berlin, Germany: Springer Science and Business Media, 2006), 8.

another case along the same lines, Las Vegas singer Wayne Newton sued a news network for defamation. The network claimed that because Newton was a public figure, he had no right to privacy. However, the court noted that the published information was wrong, and Newton won the case along with a large payout.[15]

Some standards of privacy extend beyond the law. In other words, they are not legally mandated, but many news organizations adhere to them because of their own ethics. One of these is not naming crime victims. Some members of the public think it is illegal to publish the names of crime victims, although this is not true. The reason crime victims are not named by many news outlets is that some news organizations have rules against it. For instance, it is legal to release the names of minors who have been arrested. However, many news organizations do not publish this information, even though finding out the names may be fairly easy to accomplish. This has also traditionally been the situation with rape victims. Often the rape victims' names and identities have been kept private even when they appear on the witness stand in court. This is because the news organizations have believed that a higher standard is needed than that provided by law. Another informal rule that some video news stations follow is not to show the bodies of accident victims. This is not done because of the law, but because the news organizations believe it to be a standard of good taste.[16]

These kinds of ethical standards traditionally used by news organizations are not always followed by those on the Internet. For instance, it is relatively easy to use a search engine to find an individual's address and then post the contact information. This outing of a person's personal information on the Internet is called doxing, and it is done in some cases simply because the doxed individual has an unpopular opinion. However, when internet users

---

[15] Robert Lindsey, "Carol Burnett Given $1.6 Million in Suit Against National Enquirer," *New York Times*, March 27, 1981, https://www.nytimes.com/1981/03/27/us/carol-burnett-given-1.6-million-in-suit-against-national-enquirer.html; Katherine Bishop, "Wayne Newton's Libel Award Against NBC is Overturned," *New York Times*, August 31, 1990, https://www.nytimes.com/1990/08/31/us/wayne-newton-s-libel-award-against-nbc-is-overturned.html.
[16] Ron F. Smith, *Ethics in Journalism*, 6th ed. (Malden, MA: Blackwell Publishing, 2008), 230; John Taylor, *Body Horror: Photojournalism, Catastrophe and War* (Manchester, UK: Manchester University Press, 1998), 54.

dox an individual, others may threaten and even physically attack the person whose identifying information has been released.[17]

Globally, there are differences in belief on privacy standards in regard to those who have been arrested. In the United States, arrest records are public as are court records, mug shots and the right to publish court proceedings. Therefore, a member of the public can publish the name of anyone who is arrested as long as it is said that they are only alleged to have committed the crime. While this caveat states that they have not been proven guilty, a great deal of harm can still occur by publicity from an arrest, even if the person is released and never charged. Because of this, in Canada, the rights of the accused have more protection, which is in line with European concepts of privacy that give the individual greater control of their image.[18]

In the past, determining which news organizations were legitimate was not difficult, because there were few organizations distributing news. Today, however, distinguishing between an irresponsible YouTube channel and a bona fide news YouTube channel can be a challenge. For instance, while ABC News would easily be categorized as a serious news channel, it would be more difficult to categorize some of the newer online news organizations similarly.[19]

## The Canons of Journalism: Decency

The last Canon of Journalism focuses on decency and zeroes in on making sure the public has all the truthful news requisite for providing an informed electorate capable of making decisions in a democracy. In regard to decency, the Canons of Journalism noted: "A newspaper cannot escape conviction of insincerity if while professing high moral purpose it supplies incentives to base conduct, such as are to be found in details of crime and vice, publication of which is not demonstrably for the general good."[20] Two

---

[17] Robert Trager, Susan Dente Ross, and Amy Reynolds, *The Law of Journalism and Mass Communication*, 6th ed. (Thousand Oaks, CA: CQ Press, 2018), 267.

[18] David H. Flaherty, *Protecting Privacy in Surveillance Societies: The Federal Republic of Germany, Sweden, France, Canada, and the United States* (Chapel Hill, NC: University of North Carolina Press, 2014), 246.

[19] Jim Rutenberg, "Buzzfeed News in Limbo Land," *New York Times*, January 20, 2019, https://www.nytimes.com/2019/01/20/business/media/buzzfeed-trump-mueller-backlash.html.

[20] Pratte, *Gods Within the Machine*, 206.

salient points from this canon are that it is important not to be sensational in unnecessary details and to present information that is for the public good. In past chapters we have looked at sensationalism as starting with the Penny Press Era and reaching its apex in the Yellow Journalism Era. Now we will scrutinize gatekeeping and sensationalism in regard to current relevance.

One of the ways censorship occurs today is through gatekeeping, which occurs when information providers select what specific information the public will see or hear. The term gatekeeping refers to a guard at a gate who determines what shall pass through, and in communications this refers to what information news organizations pass on to the public. Because more events happen in a news cycle than there is space or time to report, decisions have to be made regarding what stories the public will be told. This is the essence of gatekeeping theory, which holds news providers responsible for purveying information the public acquires. The problem comes when gatekeeping creates bias.[21] In the early days of printing in Europe, some printers would leave blank areas on a news sheet that had been censored as a sign to readers that material had been removed by the government who were acting as gatekeepers. It was a legal way to protest government gatekeeping without directly criticizing the government.[22]

There is little argument that information providers are gatekeepers. For instance, newspapers have the same number of pages in every issue, which means that some things have to be left out. Likewise, a traditional newscast used to have twenty-two minutes to bring the news. Regardless of how much news there was, it had to fit into twenty-two minutes. The time allotted to news was called the news hole, which had to be filled for each newscast. Actually, it was even less than twenty-two minutes, as there had to be time for sports, weather and a feel-good story known as a kicker at the end.[23] This shows that channel requirements themselves are gatekeepers and demand some material be left out. When particular items are left out because of partisanship, the gatekeeping creates a barrier to the marketplace of ideas.[24]

---

[21] Wojciech Cwalina, Andrzej Falkowski, and Bruce I. Newman, *Political Marketing: Theoretical and Strategic Foundations* (Philadelphia: Routledge, 2015), 56.
[22] "Incidents in Foreign Graphic Circles," *The Inland Printer*, Vol. 54 (Chicago: The Inland Printer Company Publishers, 1915), 504.
[23] Barbie Zelizer and Stuart Allan, *Keywords in News and Journalism Studies* (New York: Open University Press, 2010). 87.
[24] Timothy Vos and Francois Heinderyckx, *Gatekeeping in Transition* (New York: Routledge, 2015), 15.

Today, 24-hour a day news channels still have a similar news hole, and the news stories are usually repeated every half hour or hour at the most, because 24-hour news stations expect a large audience turnover. It also occurs because every minute of presented news has a high financial cost and repeating the same content saves the corporation money. The result of these factors is that only a fraction of stories that could appear on the news, actually do. If you have ever seen an event that you believed was important and were disappointed that it was not on the news, you have encountered this kind of gatekeeping.[25]

Gatekeeping is a product of the news collection process, and news producers for centuries have had to decide what the news of the day is. However, it is a very subjective selection. If a group of individuals watched a newscast, each might rate the importance of the stories differently, and the same is true with news producers whose job it is to make conscious choices as to what stories are going to see the light of day. The editorial criteria for news story selection are called news values.[26]

In order to fully understand gatekeeping, it is important to assess some foundational studies. Two analyses on gatekeeping that took place in the late 1970s by Gaye Tuchman and Herbert Gans have relevance today because they showed the impact that news organizations have on news itself.

In 1978 Tuchman wrote a book called *Making News* that explained research she had completed on how news producers work. She had conducted an ethnographic study of newsrooms in the same way sociologists study cultures. What she learned helped journalists understand their own shortcomings and assisted public relations professionals in grasping how to best communicate with journalists. Tuchman felt that women's issues and women's events were not being covered by the news organizations, so she worked to unearth information pertaining to how the news was gathered, literally scrutinizing the subculture of journalists to determine how their work patterns affected news production. One of her discoveries was that reporters have what she metaphorically called a news net. Inside the news net was the news that reporters were able to catch that day, and the methods

---

[25] Vos and Heinderyckx, *Gatekeeping in Transition*, 124.
[26] Paul Brighton and Dennis Foy, *News Values* (Thousand Oaks, CA: Sage Publications, 2007), 1.

the reporters used, she found, determined what went into the net.[27]

Tuchman discovered that an old method dating back to the Penny Press Era was affecting what news appeared in newscasts and newspapers. This was the beat system. As mentioned previously in describing the Penny Press, the beat system means that a particular reporter is in charge of one subject, and another is in charge of another subject.[28] Common reporter beats include the crime beat, the political beat and the business beat. Despite the helpfulness of the beat system in providing organization for a daily news program, Tuchman discovered a problem which was that while the beats assured a steady supply of news each day, any item that was not within the coverage area of a beat, went unreported. This caused news outlets to miss potentially important stories because the definition of news was simply what the beat system covered.[29]

Tuchman also discovered that the time when the reporter first hears about a story is important. Tuchman found reporters were eager to report stories on Monday when they were starting out fresh from the weekend. However, Friday was a bad day to send a reporter a news announcement, because the reporter was getting ready for the weekend, or had already left. This has resulted in the common practice today by public relations personnel of sending news to reporters on Monday morning to increase the likelihood it will be covered. This timing of news releases continues today in social media. Likewise, individuals today sometimes plan when they will release information on Facebook, Twitter or Instagram in order to maximize when most people are looking at their social media accounts.[30]

Related to the timing of news releases to reporters, Tuchman found that the time an individual holds an event also helps determine whether there will be news coverage. This was particularly true about the weekend. Tuchman found that most news was gathered on weekdays, and many stories that were published on the weekends, had been created earlier. Often reporters would do stories that could air at any time, and then use them on the weekend. Reporters called these non-time sensitive stories evergreen reports, because they were always usable. One of the reasons that news publishers did not assign reporters to the weekends was because that audience was less likely

---

[27] Gaye Tuchman, *Making News: A Study in the Construction of Reality* (New York: Free Press, 1978), 15.
[28] Tuchman, *Making News,* 21, 39-63.
[29] Tuchman, *Making News,* 45.
[30] Tuchman, *Making News,* 42.

to access news, and Tuchman realized that events held on a weekend were not as likely to receive coverage.[31]

Tuchman's findings still hold true today when many individuals get their news from online news sources. Many communication systems favor certain kinds of stories over others. In the digital world, this may involve computer algorithms which measure a story's success, or it may be from a built-in software function on your cell phone or a specific cell phone app.

A year after Tuchman's book was published, Herbert J. Gans published the seminal journalism book *Deciding What's News* which described the pressures that go into creating a lineup of the days' news. Gans' work emerged from a study of leading news makers at the time, showing how the selection of news stories can be both subjective and arbitrary.[32]

One news influencing factor that Gans cited was the likelihood of being sued. For example, a news producer may have important information about how a business is taking advantage of society but may not want to pay for a lawyer to affirm that they were within legal bounds of libel laws to publish the report. When investigative reporting is done in modern times, it is often about an individual who does not have the means to sue, a factor causing many stories to go unreported. Consequently, investigative reporting is interesting and may be good for society, but many news sources do not see it as profitable because of the likelihood of being sued.[33]

Time and space were another reason Gans provided to explain why many stories do not make it into the news. Gans found news producers know that most news readers and viewers are not going to spend a great deal of time on the news, and therefore present only a few stories as a result, knowing the audience members will read no more than six or seven headlines before choosing one or two to explore in more depth.[34]

There are also some stories which lend themselves to video over text. Video news producers are likely to prioritize pictures of a large fire highly because audiences are drawn to that which is visually striking. These may make the top of the list, or the first story of a newscast, even though the fire did not

---

[31] Tuchman, *Making News*, 145.

[32] Herbert J. Gans, *Deciding What's News: A Study of the CBS Evening News, NBC Nightly News, Newsweek, and Time* (Evanston, IL: Northwestern University Press, 2004), xxi.

[33] Gans, *Deciding What's News*, 263.

[34] Gans, *Deciding What's News*, 160.

affect many people. On the other hand, a video newscast may be less likely to talk about the Central Bank raising the interest rate, because it is not a visual story. Certainly, the bank story would affect potentially more people, but may not be considered an exciting story if it lacks the visual attraction.[35]

Another factor that determines what is in the news is how cheaply an event or news idea can be made into a news story. At one time there were international news bureaus all over the world, feeding stories to news cooperatives, agencies and networks at great expense. In modern times, few of these exist. Many organizations simply send a reporter to a hotspot for a day or two to show a presence there, before flying the reporter back. This is called parachute journalism, and has been criticized in the past because the reporter does not have contacts in the area, a background of the culture or time to actually explore the story. Other international stories are produced by freelancers, some of whom are professional, with others being more interested in sensational video than an accurate story.[36]

Gans revealed that another factor in deciding what will go into a newscast is the ability to get details of the story, because an event can happen, but there may be no way to confirm the details, and thus it may be excluded from a presentation of the day's news. An aspect of this element in video news is whether an event can be captured on film. The large number of cell phone cameras available today make this more likely. However, if no video is captured, the story often will not make it into the news hole. There was an old joke in broadcast journalism when this author was working in news that was a play on the slogan carpe diem, which is Latin for seize the day. Broadcast journalists would claim that their motto was carpe video, or seize the video, because the possession of video was of prime importance, and without it, there was often no story.[37]

Researchers Pam Shoemaker and Stephen Reese further studied news influences, finding that they exist on many levels, including the organizational level, which focuses on institutional pressures applied on journalists. Shoemaker and Reese demonstrated that institutions can impose pressure on journalists to produce stories with an institutional bias.[38]

---

[35] Gans, *Deciding What's News,* 158.
[36] Gans, *Deciding What's News*, 214.
[37] Gans, *Deciding What's News,* 158.
[38] Pamela J., Shoemaker and Stephen D. Reese, *Mediating the Message: Theories of Influences of Mass Media Content* (White Plains, NY: Longman, 1995), 144, 175;

Shoemaker and Reese suggested advertisers are another level of influence on the news. For instance, businesses would expect good treatment in the news if they had advertised, a news organization conflict of interest that could result in gatekeeping. In the past, some reporters would receive press releases with the initials B.O.M. (Business Office Must) written on them by the advertising sales representatives, indicating the journalist was required to do a story on a particular business because the business was an advertiser. In a few rare cases, media organizations offered advertisers news coverage for specific amounts of money, although this did not happen in the major networks. Sometimes the advertiser influence was subtler. For example, in one news program focusing on agriculture, all of the news reports showed a certain brand of tractor in the background which was recognizable from a distance by its color.[39]

Another element of influence that Shoemaker and Reese identified was the individual, suggesting that the individual prejudices present in everyone to some extent can affect a journalist's choices. For instance, a news editor who has a particular belief, may shun stories which do not go along with that belief system. This kind of gatekeeping is hard to spot, because it results in the absence of stories, and audiences literally do not know what they are missing.[40]

A hypothetical example of this kind of gatekeeping would be a news producer who is against gun control, and perhaps he or she believes any legislation against guns is a slippery slope that should not be tolerated. The news producer then selects stories for broadcast that show individuals in situations where guns have saved their lives. Assuming that the stories are completely factual and reported without bias, the result is that even though the reporting itself is not slanted, the selection of stories is, and because no stories of an opposing view are presented, the overall coverage is not balanced.

Continuing the hypothetical example given above, changes can be made to further illustrate the point. In this iteration of the hypothetical case, the news producer favors gun control, and thinks the Sixth Amendment applied only to muskets and that all other firearms should be banned. The pro-gun control news producer then selects stories for broadcast that show situations where

Shoemaker, Pamela J., and Timothy Vos, *Gatekeeping Theory* (New York: Routledge, 2009), 62.
[39] Shoemaker and Reese, *Mediating the Message*, 195.
[40] Shoemaker and Reese, *Mediating the Message*, 18.

individuals have been accidently or deliberately killed with guns. These stories may be put together in a way that does not editorialize any position, and yet the result is still an imbalance of information, as there is no completeness in either of the newscasts. From a viewer's perspective, this is difficult to ascertain, but it remains a kind of gatekeeping. There are other ways news producers deliberately use gatekeeping to promote an ideological or political position. For instance, sometimes in politics, one politician's weaknesses are emphasized, while his or her strengths are not. Just as often, a politician's weaknesses may be disregarded because of ideological motivations.[41]

The difficulty with gatekeeping is that when it occurs, individuals do not see a marketplace of ideas, a full picture of society, and their decisions are therefore not based on reality, but based on an illusion created by specifically culled stories. Columnist Walter Lippmann in *Public Opinion* wrote that the media are responsible for the "pictures in our heads."[42] For those supervising news choices, it comes down to an interesting question. Do individuals have a right to know ideas and information with which the news reporter disagrees? In a democratically free society, the answer should be in the affirmative, as journalism author John Merrill claimed: "If people have the right to know, the press has an obligation to tell them."[43]

## The Canons of Journalism: Sensationalism

While sensationalism became popular in the 1830s during the Penny Press Era, in the present-day its popularity continues with the practice of click-bait, a title or picture that entices an individual to click a link which usually doesn't live up to the title or image. The definition of sensationalism goes beyond disappointment, however. Specifically, the word sensationalism refers to reports that appeal to base instincts which usually translates to stories focusing on sex and violence more than is necessary to tell a story.[44]

---

[41] Sharon Meraz and Zizi Papacharissi, "Networked Framing and Gatekeeping," in *The Sage Handbook of Digital Journalism*, eds. Tamara Witschge, C.W. Anderson, David Domingo, and Alfred Hermida (Thousand Oaks, CA: Sage, 2016), 102-3.

[42] Walter Lippmann, *Public Opinion* (New York: Harcourt Brace and Company, Inc., 1922), 29.

[43] John C. Merrill, *The Dialectic in Journalism: Toward a Responsible Use of Press Freedom* (Baton Rouge, LA: Louisiana State University Press, 1993), 34.

[44] John D. Stevens, *Sensationalism and the New York Press* (New York: Columbia University Press, 1991), 5.

Click-bait headlines are promoted by advertisers who pay according to resultant advertising click-throughs, and if there is no action, the content creator receives no payment. Therefore, content creators are more likely to utilize sensational headlines, because they are more remunerative. This approach is similar to that of the Penny Press newspapers, which had to sell by a single headline in bold type above the fold that could be seen from a distance. Additionally, the newspaper seller would shout the headline for all to hear. In both cases of Penny Press sidewalk sales and modern click-bait, there was/is no payment without action by the consumer.[45]

This kind of enticement is built into the YouTube platform, in that the thumbnails of the videos that YouTube provides for selection may not be representative of the video, and titles can be misleading. In the instructional book *How to Do Everything with YouTube* author Chad Fahs admits that thumbnails "act as visual clues when browsing but are not always accurate depictions of what a video is about."[46] Additionally, because a viewer is not presented with an option of seeing a video clip's rating before clicking on it, the user cannot see if a video has poor ratings until after it has been clicked on. In this way the digital technology is a two-edged sword that can create a massive audience, but also financially rewards creators of sensational click-bait headlines.[47]

In competition with less scrupulous online news producers, many traditional news outlets have resorted to click-bait style headlines online and off, and even the major traditional media have admitted to succumbing to this temptation.[48] Numerous news startups including *Vox*, *Vice* and *Buzzfeed* have had little experience in traditional journalism, although *Buzzfeed* has been enthusiastic in embracing serious news and moving past its normal fare of humorous lists and pictures of animals, accumulating $850 million for its

---

[45] Jill Abramson, *Merchants of Truth: The Business of News and the Fight for Facts* (New York: Simon & Schuster, 2020), 406.
[46] Chad Fahs, *How to Do Everything with YouTube* (New York: McGraw Hill Professional, 2007), 12.
[47] Victor Pickard, *Democracy without Journalism?: Confronting the Misinformation Society* (New York: Oxford University Press, 2019), 174.
[48] Becket Adams, "The New York Times Walks Back Sensational Hurricane Irma Scare Headline Following Criticism," *Washington Examiner,* September 11, 2017, https://www.washingtonexaminer.com/the-new-york-times-walks-back-sensational-hurricane-irma-scare-headline-following-criticism; John Herman, "Self-Correcting Beyond a Web Era Marked by Sensationalism," *New York Times,* March 20, 2016, https://www.nytimes.com/2016/03/21/business/media/self-correcting-beyond-a-web-era-of-sensationalism.html.

news operation.[49]

While some sensationalism is done deliberately for monetary reasons, sometimes perceived sensationalism occurs from a difference in the value that people place on news stories. For instance, during an election, some newspapers focus almost exclusively on candidate background stories rather than their political views. In the past this has been seen as sensationalism because other stories that were important, did not get covered. Specifically, during the 2016 presidential election, the national news focused heavily on candidates. This was criticized as sensationalism because less attention was paid to other stories, such as a $400 million Obama administration payout to Iraq and a classified report showing a specific group of terrorists had doubled the number of countries in which it operated. The later story had little coverage, while other topics of arguably less importance were covered in detail.[50]

These situations call for journalists to be able to carefully investigate the real importance of a story. When news of Hillary Clinton's emails arose, many sensational stories misrepresented what investigators found. While Clinton's hacked emails released by WikiLeaks were definitely a story, some observers felt the actual content of the emails, which simply underscored the small time pettiness of some of her staffers, was blown out of proportion as to what it actually was. In contrast, when a similar incident occurred in France, French reporters were more careful with initial reports of a story concerning politician Emmanuel Macron's emails. The French press took care to look at the hacked emails and reported that there was little of importance in them. These examples show that scale is an important part of sensationalism. While many stories are worthy of being heard, hyping the importance of a story can lead to sensationalism.[51]

The root of sensationalism is in words. The words that describe something can have different strengths, and that can conflate a story. For instance, a news reporter who visits the police station to check for stories, may get a

---

[49] Jeffrey Dvorkin. "Why Click-Bait Will be the Death of Journalism," *PBS,* April 27, 2018, https://www.pbs.org/newshour/economy/what-you-dont-know-about-click-bait-journalism-could-kill-you.

[50] Joe Concha, "Presidential Race Coverage Focusing Solely on Sensationalism," *The Hill*, August 3, 2016, https://thehill.com/blogs/pundits-blog/presidential-campaign/290228-presidential-race-coverage-focusing-solely-on.

[51] David Leonhardt, "A French Lesson for the American Media," *New York Times,* May 9, 2017, https://www.nytimes.com/2017/05/09/opinion/a-french-lesson-for-the-american-media.html.

report of a simple armed robbery, which is a felony, and in many cities, it would be considered news. However, the description can take the report from news to sensationalism. The robbery can be portrayed in simple terms. However, if the headline describes it as a heist, indicating a major theft, it would become sensationalism. While the word heist might increase the likelihood that someone would read the story, credibility would be lost when the reader found the headline was misleading in regard to the scale of the crime.

We can understand the stakes of exaggeration by probing our own personal communication on social media. When individuals post a picture of a cup of coffee on Facebook, Twitter or Snapchat, they want to get as many responses as possible, so they may title the picture, "Best day ever!" Individuals expect this kind of exaggeration in casual conversation, and the stakes here are small to nonexistent because the exaggeration is recognized. The same kind of insignificant embellishment occurs with advertising. If an advertisement declares that a certain brand of mayonnaise will change the users' lives, users know it is hyperbole, and advertising laws allow this kind of puffery. However, there are different standards when the claims are taken seriously. For instance, if an individual on Facebook said they had a life-threatening disease, but a few hours later said it was just a joke, it would be considered out of the bounds of good behavior. The difference is that when an individual says something that is assumed to be a statement of fact, we presume it to be that. The stakes are high in personal communication, because individuals' reputations rise and fall on whether they are known to tell the truth. Similarly, the stakes are high when a news outlet overhypes a story, and consequently, the public becomes guarded with the source. In *Sensational Subjects*, author John Jervis notes the controversy over "whether sensationalism distorts our ability to acquire self-knowledge, to understand events around us, and to relate to others" is now two-centuries old.[52]

One of the most insidious effects of sensationalism is that it latently undermines the value of important news. When sensational stories get attention, they are given more prominence. This provides more individuals a chance to see them and they move in an upward spiral of visibility. This prominence of sensational, but often unimportant stories, lowers the opportunity for individuals to encounter serious news. An example of this was the old Facebook system for promoting news, which allowed sensational

---

[52] John Jervis, *Sensational Subjects: The Dramatization of Experience in the Modern World* (New York: Bloomsbury Academic, 2015), 1.

news, sometimes completely fabricated news, to achieve prominence.[53] Two groups of people took advantage of Facebook to promote sensational news in this manner. One was a group of Russians who operated to deliberately destabilize the 2016 election, and make Americans lose faith in the election process by operating fake accounts used to post news that appeared as serious news items.[54] Another type of individual that posted sensational and often untrue news was independent operators who generated income for themselves by creating posts which became viral.[55] Since then, Facebook officials claimed to have improved the algorithm to be more friendly to serious stories. The Facebook situation was important, because it turned out that a large percentage of people receive their news from Facebook.[56] Though these two types of actors had dissimilar motives, they both created disinformation and undermined the credibility of the democratic election process.

This chapter looked at the Canons of Journalism elements of fair play and decency, which cover the areas of privacy, gatekeeping and sensationalism. From the preceding examination and examples, it is clear that these elements address problems that are still prominent in today's media, though the means of transmission have evolved. Seeing that these and other elements from the 1923 Canons of Journalism are still a concern, the final chapter in this book will construct a new code of ethics based on these findings.

## Discussion Questions

1. Remember: Can you identify the elements of the Canons of Journalism discussed in this chapter and describe what each means?

---

[53] William E. Lee, Daxton R. Stewart, Johnathan Peters, *The Law of Public Communication* (New York: Routledge, 2017), 56.

[54] Kathleen Hall Jameson, *Cyberwar: How Russian Hackers and Trolls Helped Elect a President* (New York: Oxford University Press, 2018), 13.

[55] Whitney Phillips, *This is Why We Can't Have Nice Things: Mapping the Relationship Between Online Trolling and Mainstream Culture* (Cambridge, MA: MIT Press, 2015), 68.

[56] Laharee Chatterjee, "New York Times Beats as Digital Subscriptions Surge, Shares Rise," *Reuters*, February 8, 2018, https://www.reuters.com/article/us-new-york-times-results/new-york-times-beats-as-digital-subscriptions-surge-shares-rise-idUSKBN1FS249.

2. Understand: Why do you think the elements from the Canons of Journalism still remain as challenges today? Give several reasons why these elements are persistent challenges to journalism and free speech through the decades of changing technology.

3. Apply: Information providers are gatekeepers in that they choose what information they report on. How would you describe the difference between censorship and gatekeeping? Identify several ways those in a gatekeeping role can avoid censoring information and provide as complete a picture as possible for news consumers.

4. Evaluate: Discuss with others how they define privacy and how much they value it on a scale from one to ten, with one being the least and ten being the most. What differences in definition and valuation did you find? What factors do you believe influence how a person perceives privacy and how much they value it?

5. Create: Write a short essay which describes a standard of work to avoid sensationalism, referencing modern technology. In what ways is it different from what the Canons of Journalism suggested?

# CHAPTER EIGHT

# A PROPOSED CODE OF ETHICS FOR MODERN MEDIA

In previous chapters this book examined the Canons of Journalism both historically and in regard to how they might apply in modern times, creating a foundation for this final chapter, which discusses forming a modern code of journalism ethics that applies to the communication problems and challenges in modern times. From this discussion a proposed code of ethics will be constructed.

Constructing a new journalism code of ethics requires understanding what is at stake for society. While laws have given traditional journalists extra consideration because of the high value society places on free speech, earlier discussion noted that for every right there is a corresponding responsibility, and the code of ethics is therefore meant as a guideline to journalists' responsibilities. We have reviewed the responsibilities from the Canons of Journalism in regard to their history and current state, and so the task at hand is to evaluate whether any or all of those can still apply to the modern day cultural and technological landscape. Furthermore, examination extends to whether new technology has caused any new challenges.

The new code of ethics will not cover every situation, but it will provide general guidelines under which ethical communicators can function with some level of confidence, as well as aid the general public in understanding the limitations under which modern communicators, journalists and de facto journalists operate. Earlier in this book, nineteenth century events were discussed in relation to the formation of standards of work, which evolved into codes of ethics in the twentieth century. The catalyst for the standards of work was the Industrial Revolution, which spurred the creation of the mass media through technological innovation including faster printing presses and means of distribution. As described in the beginning of this book, the mass media created new audiences and approaches to spreading

news, starting with a period of time called the Penny Press, when newspapers
1targeted the common person rather than elites.[1]

The new kind of newspaper created challenges that some journalists felt
would be solved with the formation of an expert class of workers. They
envisioned journalism as a profession, which at the time was seen as a vital
societal office, carrying heavy responsibilities like the other professions at
the time, doctors, lawyers and the clergy. These were distinguished as
having organizations, university training and codes of ethics.[2]

It was this emphasis on professions that compelled journalists to create the
first university schools of journalism, professional organizations and codes
of professional conduct. The American Society of Newspaper Editors
adapted a code of ethics early in 1923, and the elements of these Canons of
Journalism were widely used as codes of ethics in the last half of the
nineteenth century.[3]

One of the purposes of this book was to determine if the Canons of
Journalism elements still apply in today. Therefore, this chapter will start
by analyzing Chapters Five, Six, and Seven, which examined the Canons of
Journalism elements in light of recent history and current media. We will
continue with an examination of three foundations of journalism, the need
for a code of ethics and finally a presentation of a new code of ethics.

## Responsibility and Independence

Chapter Five looked at the Canons of Journalism elements of responsibility
and independence. It was noted that responsibility has been a relatively rare
commodity in both traditional and digital media, as early breaches of
societally appropriate material and sometimes even criminal conduct left
little doubt in the public mind that media outlets were not always operating
in the public's best interests.[4]

---

[1] Sidney Kobre, *Development of American Journalism* (Dubuque, IA: Wm. C.
Brown Company Publishers, 1969), 314-15.
[2] Howard M. Vollmer and Donald L. Mills, *Professionalization* (Englewood Cliffs,
NJ: Prentice-Hall Inc., 1966), 2.
[3] Paul Alfred Pratte, *Gods Within the Machine: A History of the American Society
of Newspaper Editors, 1923-1993* (Westport, CT: Praeger, 1995), 205-6.
[4] Edwin Emery and Michael Emery, *The Press and America* (Upper Saddle River,
NJ: Prentice Hall, 1984), 194.

In examining independence, it was revealed that the 1947 Hutchins Commission proposed that the government have more control over journalism, a suggestion that many journalists opposed because of its potential to undermine the First Amendment. Then in the 1980s, President Ronald Reagan deregulated broadcasting which changed the landscape of televised news, as news stations were no longer required to follow strict FCC rules on news coverage, and the growth of cable news made FCC rules moot. Deregulation thus led to increased partisanship and a concentration of ownership, diminishing the number of independent voices.[5]

In the 2000s, the Internet became a dominant news conduit, producing both opportunities and challenges. The power of individual news magnets such as Ted Turner and Rupert Murdoch in the West and the controlling structure of governments such as China in the East caused individuals to question whether impartiality is even possible in many modern media environments.[6]

## Sincerity, Truthfulness, Accuracy and Impartiality

Chapter Six followed up with four more elements from the Canons of Journalism: sincerity, truthfulness, accuracy and impartiality. These elements may be summarized in the modern problem of information fabrication, inventing stories and presenting them as truth. Not only has the media continued to have this problem since the time the Canons of Journalism included it as a threat to journalism in 1923, it may even have increased because of the ability of bad actors to simulate credible stories, while social media users indiscriminately share questionable information until it becomes viral. This concern is supported by research suggesting that false news tweets are shared six times more on average than truthful ones.[7]

This element saw a resurgence on social media in the run up to the 2016 United States Presidential Election, as false reports were deliberately spread on social media for financial gain, to help a particular party and to spread confusion in general. The fact that Russia was involved was not surprising

---

[5] John C. Merrill, *The Imperative of Freedom: A Philosophy of Journalistic Autonomy* (New York: Hastings House Publishers, 1974), 36; Jennifer Holt, *Empires of Entertainment: Media Industries and the Politics of Deregulation, 1980-1996* (New Brunswick, NJ: Rutgers University Press, 2011), 69.
[6] Paul J. Bolt and Sharyl N. Cross, *China, Russia and Twenty-First Century Global Geopolitics* (Oxford, UK: Oxford University Press, 2018), 219.
[7] Robert J. Shiller, *Narrative Economics: How Stories Go Viral and Drive Major Economic Events* (Princeton, NJ: Princeton University Press, 2019), 96.

as Russia, and previously the Soviet Union, had long participated in disinformation campaigns. The surprising component was how successful Russian operatives were with social media and the facility with which the public was swayed by hoaxes.[8]

Earlier in this book, it was noted that the Canons of Journalism's concern for accuracy was seen to be in as great a danger as ever in contemporary times as anonymity of the Internet makes it difficult to access a source's identity, much less its credibility. Additionally, an absence of corporate self-policing and government regulation undermines the veracity of online journalism. Anonymous bad actors can disseminate false statements and face no recrimination because their identities are secret. This is something news organizations cannot do, because they are expected to be responsible and will lose credibility if their information is found to be untruthful.[9]

In regard to impartiality, conflict of interest was also discussed, and was found to be excessive in modern media. This was discovered to be prevalent in self-published formats like blogs and vlogs, which may recommend products they have secretly been paid to promote, as well as traditional media organizations which tout the virtues of products from sister companies in their corporate families.[10] However, it can also play an insidious influence on journalists through the latent threat of a loss of sponsorship if a report harmful to the sponsors is published.[11]

---

[8] Todd C. Helmus, Elizabeth Bodine-Baron, Andrew Radin, Madeline Magnuson, Joshua Mendelsohn, William Marcellino, Andriy Bega, and Zev Winkelman, *Russian Social Media Influence: Understanding Russian Propaganda in Eastern Europe* (n. p.: Rand Corporation, 2018), 7, 27.

[9] Denis McQuail, *McQuail's Mass Communication Theory* (Thousand Oaks, CA: Sage, 2005), 382.

[10] Ric Jensen, in "Blogola, Sponsored Posts, and the Ethics of Blogging," *The Ethics of Emerging Media*, eds. Bruce E. Drushel and Kathleen German (New York: The Continuum International Publishing Group, 2011), 219; Mark Tremayne, "Harnessing the Active Audience: Synthesizing Blog Research and Lessons for the Future of Media," in *Blogging, Citizenship, and the Future of Media*, ed. Mark Tremayne (New York: Routledge, 2012), 264.

[11] Bob Franklin and Mark Hanna, "Advertising," in *Key Concepts in Journalism Studies*, eds., Bob Franklin, Martin Hamer, Hark Hanna, Marie Kinsey, and John E. Richardson (Thousand Oaks, CA: Sage, 2005), 9.

## Fair Play and Decency

The last two elements in the Canons of Journalism examined earlier were fair play and decency, which broach the areas of privacy, gatekeeping and sensationalism, covered in Chapter Seven. Invasions of privacy were found to be excessive in modern times as details of private individuals have become easier to obtain and disseminate, often anonymously, although one argument suggests that individuals' lives are now less private than in times past and because they willingly live more openly. The real question becomes whether individuals have a right to keep secrets in a transparent, or at the least translucent, culture.[12] While the level of desired privacy differs according to individuals and cultures, there is a basic right to some privacy as implied in the Constitution, and the question is simply how much.[13] This is an area where technology has changed aspects of the original concern, in that when the Canons of Journalism first talked about privacy, it was not referring to modern problems of harassment and doxing protected by the Internet's anonymity.[14]

The Canons of Journalism element of gatekeeping continues to be a challenge, even though the structure of communication dissemination has changed, where today a communicator with only a YouTube channel and virtually no overhead costs may attain more subscribers than any newspaper chain did when the Canons of Journalism were written. However, individual publishers today are also involved in gatekeeping as they select items for dissemination that they believe will generate the most attention and profit. Additionally, many news outlets are merely aggregating news that they glean from the few original newsgathering publishers that still exist, and while there are numerous news sites, they are in fact repeating what a diminishing number of reporters have published. Those reporters who do original reporting have an increased gatekeeping ability because what they decide is news will have an impact far beyond their own news organization's ability to publish. This is why, beyond the purview of a code

---

[12] Adam D. Moore, *Privacy Rights: Moral and Legal Foundations* (University Park, PA: Penn State Press, 2010), 87.
[13] Andrew McStay, *Privacy and the Media* (Los Angeles: Sage Publications, 2017), 28.
[14] Saul Levmore, "The Internet's Anonymity Problem," in *The Offensive Internet: Speech, Privacy and Reputation edited by* Saul Levmore and Martha Nussbaum (Cambridge, MA: Harvard University Press, 2010), 50, 58-9.

of ethics, the major social media companies have increasingly controlled what individuals see and hear.[15]

The last element deals with sensationalism, a journalistic technique that has been honed to a fine edge in modern times, as click-bait and deceiving headlines have become common, rather than the exception on the Internet, and into which even some prominent traditional media have strayed. A story can be presented in a riveting manner, without it appealing to baser instincts. Unfortunately, publishing sensational stories now, as in the time since the 1830s, is financially remunerative, and sensational accounts on the Internet today may be building as many mansions as they did when yellow press barons reigned in the nineteenth century.

To summarize Chapters 5 through 7, we can say that the ethical problems challenging journalists in the 1920s are still extant, and perhaps more persistent. When the authors of the Canons of Journalism created their code of ethics, they hoped it would curb journalistic excesses, and it may have. In modern times, when we find journalism excesses so common that it is often difficult to determine where ethical journalism actually exists, it might be reasoned that the Canons of Journalism have ultimately failed. Alternately, perhaps the lapse in responsibility is more appropriately placed on those journalists who have forgotten the codes of the past, and the public, in neglecting to be the informed electorate required of a democracy.

Even though individuals in modern times do not live in the same world as communicators did in the nineteenth and beginning of the twentieth centuries, communicators currently have the same pressures regarding news. For instance, in the nineteenth and twentieth centuries, publishers did not have anonymity, which in modern times creates difficulties in locating bad actors who are circulating false information. However, there were still problems in the past regarding newspapers circulating false information, because while technology changes, human motivations do not, and for every journalist trying to tell the truth, there are other communicators solely out to profit off of the information industry. Where the bottom line is the highest goal, truth will only win when it is more profitable than falsehood.

---

[15] Pamela J. Shoemaker and Timothy Vos, *Gatekeeping Theory* (New York: Routledge, 2009), 59, 60; Pamela Shoemaker, "A New Gatekeeping Model," in *Social Meanings of News*, ed. Daniel A. Berkowitz (Thousand Oaks, CA: Sage, 1997), 57.

Earlier in this book we discussed how communication technology in the Penny Press Era relied on steam, whereas communication technology in modern times relies on microchips and binary code.[16] This advance in technology seems not to have affected communication ethics for the better, and in the case of providing anonymity to offenders, for the worse.[17] The fact that the mass media gives individuals a great deal of power through influence and financial gain was the catalyst for journalism ethics using any kind of technology that disseminates information quickly. For this reason, in constructing a code of ethics, the foundations must be those of enduring values, specifically equality, truth-telling and freedom. When communication is guided by those principles the technology becomes secondary, whether the means of transmission are steam presses or smart phones.

## A Search for Standards

A fundamental question that must be asked in this chapter, is whether a code of ethics is needed. A century ago when journalists were pondering this, the concept of having professionals performing the work of experts for society was a popular ideal. However, society has largely moved past that professional model as a solution. Consequently, it could be suggested that professional codes of ethics are no longer needed in a society that views a professional class with skepticism. In a world where the word professional is applied to hairdressers, taxicab drivers and wait staff, the notion that a professional class is an elite group that must have autonomy, university education, a national organization and a code of ethics appears outdated.[18]

The professional concept has passed its golden years, and while not completely depleted, it is in its twilight stage, as the traditional professions of doctors, lawyers and the clergy have lost their veneer of invincibility as the vanguards of society who can do no wrong. The concept that society needed an expert class of people to run it, has perhaps itself run its course, as the disadvantages of this arrangement became evident in the last century, the public realizing that those who are given great responsibility do not

---

[16] David S. Landes, *The Unbound Prometheus* (Cambridge, UK: Press Syndicate of the University of Cambridge, 1969), 104.

[17] Scott Shane, "The Fake Americans Russia Created to Influence the Election," *New York Times*, September 7, 2017, https://www.nytimes.com/2017/09/07/us/politics/russia-facebook-twitter-election.html.

[18] Silvio Waisbord, *Reinventing Professionalism: Journalism and News in Global Perspective* (Malden, MA: Polity Press, 2013), 47.

always act responsibly. As a result, we have seen laws and regulations, external to professional organizations, accrue as barriers to professional excess. The trappings of professionalism from a century ago, when it was thought of as an elitist class, seem anachronistic today and if we want to put foundations under the ethical norms we adopt, we need to dig deeper than a desire to achieve an archaic status that no longer exists.[19] This does not mean abandoning a code of ethics, rather it suggests that a code is as valuable as it ever was for society in general and journalism in particular.

Today's code of ethics' raison d'être is that it is communitarian, whether that community is defined as a small circle of geographically close associates or global humanity at large. In either of these cases, standards are set for what is acceptable and tolerable, based on community values and mores. The challenge in a pluralistic system where many belief systems exist is in finding standards compatible with a gamut of belief systems. While most belief systems, inclusive of libertine positions, support some kinds of censorship, different value systems maintain distinctive criteria. For instance, one group may favor censoring depictions of violence, whereas another may believe violent portrayals are needed to communicate the truth of a situation.

Earlier we discussed journalism's role in society and its importance to democracy, but if we indeed want democracy, and believe, even in its imperfect form that it is better than tyrannical rule, than we need journalism that protects free speech. Metaphorically, journalism can be thought of as a nutrient that keeps democracy growing, but, if the public is complacent and fails to cultivate democracy, it will die of neglect. There are many nutrients for democracy, but one of the most important in the complex society in which we find ourselves is a free and responsible media.[20]

Another advantage of a code of ethics is having internal versus external control. The essential motivation of profiting off of the information industry will continue as long as there is mass media, and for this reason, for the preservation of society, there must be controls on information. The question then becomes, will the measures of control be internal or external? External controls would come from the government and would further the Constitution's protection of individual citizens from harm, specifically the

---

[19] Waisbord, *Reinventing Professionalism*, 47.
[20] C. Edwin Baker, *Media, Markets and Democracy* (New York: Cambridge University Press, 2004), 157.

right to pursue happiness, although at the cost of freedom of speech, while a code of ethics would serve as an internal control.[21]

In the past, the government has stepped in when industries failed to operate in the public interest, a situation that was particularly evident in the Progressive Era, when government agencies were formed to regulate excesses in the medical and food industries. Later, in the 1970s the FCC banned tobacco companies from advertising cigarettes on broadcast television.[22] This ruling was a concern to the makers of distilled spirits (hard liquor) because they assumed that their product was next on the list to be banned from television advertising. As a result, they voluntarily withdrew advertising on broadcast television, a condition which lasted for decades until the distilled spirits producers tested a few ads on broadcast television with success, and they began more vigorous advertising in that medium again.[23]

The United States Congress has recently expressed interest in the possibility of regulating companies such as Facebook and Google. While this does not initially seem like a threat to journalism, it begins a slippery slope which could extend to all communication. Congressional members have a point, as some regulation needs to be practiced, although it would be better to have this proceed internally rather than externally, and a resurgence in ethical conduct could provide the needed balance.[24]

## Three Foundations

In creating a code of ethics, it is important to anticipate and address a variety of modern concerns. Therefore, several vital foundations should be considered. These underlying social mores include the equality of individuals in society, truth-telling and freedom.

---

[21] McQuail, *McQuail's Mass Communication Theory,* 175-76.

[22] Stuart N. Brotman, *Communications Law and Practice* (New York: Law Journal Press, 2006), 13.

[23] Stuart Elliott, "Liquor Industry Ends Its Ad Ban in Broadcasting," *New York Times*, November 8, 1996, https://www.nytimes.com/1996/11/08/business/liquor-industry-ends-its-ad-ban-in-broadcasting.html.

[24] Mike Isaac, "Mark Zuckerberg's Call to Regulate Facebook, Explained," *New York Times,* March 30, 2019, https://www.nytimes.com/2019/03/30/technology/mark-zuckerberg-facebook-regulation-explained.html.

One commonality in many modern communities is a belief in equality of persons, although exactly what this means and how it is expressed has quite a range and continues to evolve. In ancient Greece all citizens could vote, but the Greek citizens still enslaved individuals. Therefore, while Greece professed a kind of liberty, it was not the more expansive definition of liberty most individuals today would understand.[25] The Greek version of equality extended to citizens of city states, but not to non-citizens, particularly those whom had been enslaved.[26] In more recent times Enlightenment philosophers elaborated and expanded on what equality meant, extending it beyond parochial borders of citizenship. While Enlightenment principles undergirded the formation of the United States Constitution, there was still a long way to go in regard to practicing what it preached. This was evident from the system of enslaving individuals that was in operation at the time the Constitution was ratified and in the initial lack of voting rights for all but males who owned property. This is sometimes described as a lack of universal suffrage, which most today understand as being incompatible with liberty.[27]

In modern times individuals still disagree on some aspects of equality. If there is agreement in the basic equality of rights, then it can be said that communication should benefit individuals equally. A founding principle of the Constitution was that people should be equally protected from the government, requiring individuals to be vigilant. This was perceived as requiring freedom of speech, in essence a vehicle for maintaining equality, and from this reasoning the First Amendment was created. Therefore, a code of ethics providing a foundation for truthful journalism is a force for independence from government control, and protects citizens from tyrannical leaders, should one arise.[28]

Non-democratic countries by definition do not hold the belief that citizens are the government's catalyst and therefore do not recognize a logical necessity for citizens to be in control. For instance, in the past many European countries believed in the divine right of kings, a concept that said

---

[25] George Grote, *History of Greece* (London: John Murray, 1851), 200.

[26] Matthew Dillon and Lynda Garland, *Ancient Greece: Social and Historical Documents from Archaic Times to the Death of Socrates* (New York: Routledge, 2000), 360.

[27] Peter H. Lindert, *Growing Public: Social Spending and Economic Growth Since the Eighteenth Century* (New York: Cambridge University Press, 2006), 107.

[28] John V. Pavlik, *Journalism and the New Media* (New York: Columbia University Press, 2001), 23.

God had ordained kings to rule and all others to serve them without question. This belief was in contradiction to the Enlightenment belief of equality which held that rulers should serve the people.[29]

The above example is the reason that understanding foundational belief systems is crucial to standards of conduct, as those systems influence a code's constructions. A journalism standard of work under the divine right of kings would demand allegiance to the king regardless of the truth, and no concern for informing the citizens about the government. It is understood then that the code that will be formed in this chapter will be founded on the concepts of individuals having rights and all people being equal.[30] If that was not a foundation, then a code would not be necessary because the government would be telling the media what to disseminate by fiat and there would be no need for an informed electorate.[31]

A second foundational principle is truth-telling, which is the basis for credibility.[32] To understand the need for trust, a small unit of society can be considered. Consider a village where crops are traded for tools, and trust is vital between the farmer and the merchant in order to sustain continuing transactions, without which the community breaks apart. The same principle operates in modern society where individuals must trust online marketers such as eBay and Amazon to deliver goods after a payment through a credit card or PayPal. While the modern transaction is exponentially more technically complex, it is still dependent on the primitive principle of trust. In the same manner, trust is also a pillar of societal communication in that without it, societal groups fall apart, because communication undergirds the basics requisite to live.[33]

---

[29] Stephen Eric Bronner, *Reclaiming the Enlightenment: Toward a Politics of Radical Engagement* (New York: Columbia University Press, 2004), 62.

[30] James A. Curry, Richard B. Riley, and Richard M. Battistoni, *Constitutional Government: The American Experience* (Dubuque, IA: Kendall Hunt Publishing, 2003), 183.

[31] Aaron Quinn, *Virtue Ethics and Professional Journalism* (New York: Springer Publishing, 2018), 49.

[32] Robert I. Wakefield, and Coleman F. Barney, "Communication in an Unfettered Marketplace: Ethical Interrelations of Business, Government, and Stakeholders," *Journal of Mass Media Ethics*, 16, no. 2 & 3 (2001), 229.

[33] Kees Brants, "Trust, Cynicism, and Responsiveness: The Uneasy Situation of Journalism and Democracy," in *Rethinking Journalism: Trust and Participation in a Transformed News Landscape*, eds. Chris Peters and Marcel Jeroen Broersma (New York: Routledge, 2013), 16.

## The New Code

With a belief in the need for responsible journalism in modern times and a conviction that a code of ethics would be a step in that direction, the construction of a code of ethics commences. The current items in this code of ethics reflect the concerns from the original Canons of Journalism in description, if not in exact words used to describe certain challenges. For instance, the original Canons of Journalism used the words fair play and decency which are not used prolifically in this book because modern words that more closely describe what the original creators intended are now available. For instance, decency was originally used to describe what today we call sensationalism, and that is how it has been described in this book. Likewise, the canon of fair play actually encompasses situations such as privacy and so the word privacy is used to clarify its meaning. Additionally, freedom of speech was one of the original canons, but it is excluded here for two reasons: 1) freedom of speech is implicit in what the code of ethics states, and 2) while the modern journalist is dependent on freedom of speech as a foundation, it is not actually a prescription to which a journalist can adhere. The following elements comprise a proposed code of ethics for the twenty-first century:

1. *Responsibility* means performing a duty. In the past it was said that public communicators had responsibility because the public trusted the media to give it the information needed to be an informed electorate, the basis of a democratic society. While there is a shortage of trust in the media, there is still a responsibility to create a place for the acquisition of reliable information. There is also a basic societal need to trust communication, whether it is about the government, or the world around us. Therefore, responsibility for journalists means realizing they have a larger purpose than simply providing information, advocating a position or selling a product. Truthful communication contributes to the good of society, fulfilling a duty to democracy and humanity. In practicing responsibility, journalists cannot merely follow a catalog of prescriptions, but rather let the ethos of duty pervade their actions. In short, the journalist must be truthful in order to promote equality and freedom to restore democracy and preserve humanity.

2. Communicators should create news *impartially*, without *bias* and *conflicts of interest*. If conflicts of interest exist, communicators should recuse themselves from writing about the topic, or state transparently the nature of the conflict to the news consumer. In the case of an opinion piece, the communicator should specify that they

are not purveying news, being objective and showing all sides, but rather taking an advocacy stance. While individuals may produce both unbiased communication and advocacy pieces, they should never be in the same report, commentary should not be confused with journalism and each kind of information should be specifically identified. Additionally, in presenting aggregated information, the communicator should attempt to include the original source of the report, so that the item's potential bias can be judged by weighing the source's credibility.

3. *Accuracy* of a story has previously been supported by having more than one source for a story and verifying what sources say. Using search engines for information can provide surprising results and excellent background information, but not the full story. Therefore, the journalist should realize that interviews, though time consuming, are a tested way to distill the truth. Likewise, crowdsourced stories are as reliable as the least credible person in the pool of anonymous contributors, and can be used as a possible lead, but not as a finished story.

4. The journalist should avoid *fabrication* by doing everything possible to verify the truth of a received report, including having a confirmed source. Note that simply publishing a rumor with the caveat that it has not been confirmed is not the same as doing background work. Journalists should realize that bad actors today will still try to use the journalist's credibility to sell false stories.

5. *Privacy* is a vital element for journalists to guard. Cultural proclivities toward personal transparency may continue, but regardless of definitional deviations, there will always be a necessity to protect the privacy of those who have not thrust themselves into the spotlight. Regardless of the swiftness of technology, and the imperative to publish, private individuals who wish to remain so should be allowed to have privacy. There may be extenuating circumstances, for instance in cases where individuals have public social media accounts which highlight the details of their lives, but privacy in the home is a starting point. In regard to arrests, in the United States it has been a tradition not to name crime victims unless they choose to make their situation public, and this continues to be a beneficial practice, despite the fact that some in recent times have suggested circumstances where an unfair situation can occur. Publicizing the names of minors in crimes is legal for the media in the United States, but traditionally not done by the media. This continues to be a reasonably ethical stance and is so accepted by the public that many

individuals in the public believe it is the law. The journalist should also realize there is a difference between someone who is a public figure and someone who wishes to be left alone. No individual should have their personal data such as phone number, address, etc., exposed as in the practice of doxing, which enables vigilantes to enact extra-judicial punishment in contradiction to the rule of law. The battling concepts of privacy and the people's right to know must continue to be debated in light of the Constitution and democratic principles as new conditions and technology arises.

6. *Gatekeeping* occurs, regardless of one's position as a journalist. Gatekeeping cannot be eliminated in public communication, but it should be monitored to control bias and partiality. Editors who practice information aggregation should take note both of the reports they publish and those they do not, as a way to monitor and avoid unconscious favoritism in the editing process.

7. *Sensationalism* insidiously erodes democracy's ability to work by draining credibility in public journalism. It should be avoided both in regard to over dependence on topics which are sensational by their nature and in writing legitimate stories in a sensational manner. The latter is often accomplished through sensational headlines, exaggerating the actual facts, a practice that is known online as clickbait. When the public realizes that a headline does not match the story, they may feel deceived and credibility can be lost.

In reading the previous code of ethics it may be noted that the principles are similar to the 1923 code, and that is because the ethical principles of equality, truth-telling and freedom have not changed, even though the way they must be applied has been monumentally altered because of new technology. In this code, today's challenges have been specifically described including anonymous sources, hidden sponsorships, reporting based on search engine results, doxing, news aggregation and click-bait. The reader may encounter other problems as well, and in the future new ethical dilemmas will occur. However, unless additional foundational ethical principles emerge, the elements included here will remain of value.

# Discussion Questions

1. Remember: Identify all the elements from the Canons of Journalism and explain what they prescribe.

2. Understand: Discuss which of the elements seem the most prominent in media today and which seem the least. Why do you think some are more prominent today?

3. Apply: Identify at least two elements which are essential for society. Why do you think these are important? Explain your reasons.

4. Evaluate: The right to privacy conflicts with the concept of the people's right to know. How would you defend a journalist who has published photos from a Facebook page without the owner's permission? How would you respond if the person whose Facebook pictures had been published had not thrust themselves into the spotlight?

5. Create: How you would convince a skeptical friend of the value of a code of ethics? Describe a least three reasons a code of ethics is valuable. If you are in a group, compare your response with others in your group.

# BIBLIOGRAPHY

Abramson, Jill. *Merchants of Truth: The Business of News and the Fight for Facts.* New York: Simon & Schuster, 2020.

Abrahamson, Mark. *Functionalism.* Upper Saddle River, NJ: Prentice-Hall, 1978.

Acosta, Jim. *The Enemy of the People: A Dangerous Time to Tell the Truth in America.* New York: Harper, 2019.

Adams, Becket. "The New York Times Walks Back Sensational Hurricane Irma Scare Headline Following Criticism." *Washington Examiner.* September 11, 2017. https://www.washingtonexaminer.com/the-new-york-times-walks-back-sensational-hurricane-irma-scare-headline-following-criticism.

Adams, John to James Lloyd. February 11, 1815. In *The Works of John Adams*, edited by Charles Francis Adams, 116. Vol. 10. Boston: Little, Brown, 1851.

Adams, Samuel Hopkins. *The Great American Fraud.* Chicago: American Medical Association, 1905.

Agger, Ben. *Oversharing: Presentations of Self in the Internet Age.* New York: Routledge, 2015.

Aitamurto, Tanja. "Crowdsourcing in Open Journalism: Benefits, Challenges, and Value Creation." In *The Routledge Companion to Digital Journalism Studies*, edited by Bob Franklin and Scott A. Eldridge III, 185-193. New York: Routledge, 2018.

Allen, Charles L. *Canons of Journalism, Adopted by the American Society of Newspaper Editors in Convention 1925* [sic]. Urbana, IL: University of Illinois Studio Press, 1928.

Altschull, Herbert J. *Agents of Power.* White Plains, NY: Longman, 1984.

Amar, Vikram. *The First Amendment, Freedom of Speech: Its Constitutional History and Contemporary Debate.* Amherst, NY: Prometheus Books, 2009.

Aucoin, James L. *The Evolution of American Investigative Journalism.* Columbia, MO: University of Missouri Press, 2006.

Auletta, Ken. *Media Man: Ted Turner's Improbable Empire.* New York: W. W. Norton & Company, 2004.

Bagdikian, Ben H. *Media Monopoly.* Boston: Beacon Press, 2000.

Baker, C. Edwin. *Media Concentration and Democracy: Why Ownership Matters.* New York: Cambridge University Press, 2006.

Baker, C. Edwin. *Media, Markets and Democracy*. New York: Cambridge University Press, 2004.

Banning, Stephen A. "The Cradle of Professional Journalistic Education in the Mid-Nineteenth Century." *Journalism History Monographs* 4, no. 1 (2000) [Online serial]. http://www.scripps.ohiou.edu/mediahistory.

Banning, Stephen A. "'Determined to Suppress Everything Like Free Speech': Lincoln's Private Letters Reveal Aggressive Use of Newspaper Censorship." *Journalism History* 45, no. 1 (Spring 2020): 1-18.

Banning, Stephen A. "Fully Conscious of Their Power: Nineteenth Century Michigan Editors Search for Journalistic Professionalism." *American Journalism* 36, no. 3 (Fall 2019): 1-24.

Banning, Stephen A. "John McCutcheon's Asian Adventure: A Nineteenth-Century Adventure Journalist Covers the Battle for Manila Bay from the Inside." *Journalism History* 42, no. 1 (Spring 2016): 31-40.

Banning, Stephen A. "The Maine Press Association Takes a Stand: Promoting Professional Identity in the Nineteenth Century." *Maine Historical Journal*. Forthcoming.

Banning, Stephen A. "Not Quite Professional: Bohemian and Elitist Newspaper Clubs in Nineteenth Century Chicago." *Journalism History* 40, no. 1 (Spring 2014): 2-28.

Banning, Stephen A. "Press Clubs Champion Journalism Education." In *Journalism 1908: Birth of a Profession,* edited by Betty Winfield, 65-81. Columbia, MO: University of Missouri Press, 2008.

Banning, Stephen A. "The Professionalization of Journalism: A Nineteenth-Century Beginning." *Journalism History* 24, no. 4 (Winter 1998-1999): 157-160.

Banning, Stephen A. "Truth is Our Ultimate Goal." *American Journalism* 16, no. 1 (Winter 1999): 17-39.

Banning, Stephen A. "Unearthing the Origin of Journalistic Professionalization in the Mid-Nineteenth Century." Master's thesis, University of Missouri, 1993.

Barrett, J. W. ed. *History and Transactions of the Editors and Publishers Association of Missouri: 1867-1876.* Canton, MO: Canton Press Print, 1876.

Benkler, Yochai, Robert Faris and Hal Roberts. *Network News Propaganda: Manipulation, Disinformation, and Radicalization in American Politics.* New York: Oxford University Press, 2018.

Bennett, F. O. *History of the Press Club of Chicago.* Chicago: H. O. Shepard & Co., Printers, 1888.

Berman, David Elliot. "Breaking Babel: A Comparative Historical Analysis of Yellow Journalism and Clickbait." Paper presented at the AEJMC 2018 annual conference, Washington, DC, 6-9 Aug. 2018.

Birkhead, Douglas. "The Power in the Image: Professionalism and the Communications Revolution." *American Journalism* 1, no. 2 (Winter 1984): 1-14.

Bivens, Rena. *Digital Currents: How Technology and the Public are Shaping News.* Toronto, Canada: University of Toronto Press, 2014.

Blanchard, Margaret A. "The Hutchins Commission: The Press and the Responsibility Concept." *Journalism Monographs* 49 (May 1977).

Bleyer, Willard Grosvenor. *Main Currents in the History of American Journalism.* Boston: Houghton Mifflin, 1927.

Bolt, Paul J., and Sharyl N. Cross, *China, Russia and Twenty-First Century Global Geopolitics.* Oxford, UK: Oxford University Press, 2018.

Bostrom, Bert. *Talent, Truth and Energy: Society of Professional Journalists Sigma Delta Chi.* Chicago: Society of Professional Journalists, 1984.

Bovee, Warren G. *Discovering Journalism.* Westport, CT: Greenwood Press, 1999.

Boyer, Paul S. *Purity in Print: Book Censorship in America from the Gilded Age to the Computer Age.* Madison, WI: University of Wisconsin Press, 2002.

Bradlee, Ben. *The Good Life: Newspapering and Other Adventures.* New York: Simon Schuster, 2017.

Brake, Laurel, and Maryso Demour, eds. *Dictionary of Nineteenth Century Journalism: In Great Britain and Ireland.* London: Academia Press, 2009.

Brants, Kees. "Trust, Cynicism, and Responsiveness: The Uneasy Situation of Journalism and Democracy." In *Rethinking Journalism: Trust and Participation in a Transformed News Landscape*, edited by Chris Peters and Marcel Jeroen Broersma, 15-27. New York: Routledge, 2013.

Brighton, Paul, and Dennis Foy. *News Values.* Thousand Oaks, CA: Sage Publications, 2007.

Brock, George. *The Right to be Forgotten: Privacy and the Media in the Digital Age.* New York: I. B. Taurus & Co., 2016.

Bromwich, Jonah Engel. "Logan Paul, YouTube Video Star Says Posting of Suicide Video was 'Misguided.'" *New York Times.* January 2, 2018. https://www.nytimes.com/2018/01/02/business/media/logan-paul-youtube.html.

Bronner, Stephen Eric. *Reclaiming the Enlightenment: Toward a Politics of Radical Engagement.* New York: Columbia University Press, 2004.

Brooks, Brian S., George Kennedy, Daryl R. Moen and Don Ranly, *News Reporting and Writing*. Boston: Bedford/St. Martin's, 2011.

Brotman, Stuart N. *Communications Law and Practice*. New York: Law Journal Press, 2006.

Bugeja, Michael J. *Living Ethics: Developing Values in Mass Communication*. Boston: Allyn & Bacon, 1996.

Bynum, W. F. *Science and the Practice of Medicine in the Nineteenth Century*. New York: Cambridge University Press, 1996.

Byrum, Kristie. *The European Right to be Forgotten: The First Amendment Enemy*. New York: Lexington Books, 2018.

Calhoun, Daniel. *Professional Lives in America*. Cambridge: Harvard University Press, 1965.

Campbell, W. Joseph. *Yellow Journalism: Puncturing the Myths, Defining the Legacies*. Westport, CT: Praeger Press, 2001.

Carr-Saunders, A.M., and P.A. Wilson. *The Professions*. 2nd ed. London: Frank Cass & Co. Ltd., 1964.

Chatterjee, Laharee. "New York Times Beats as Digital Subscriptions Surge, Shares Rise." *Reuters*. February 8, 2018. https://www.reuters.com/article/us-new-york-times-results/new-york-times-beats-as-digital-subscriptions-surge-shares-rise-idUSKBN1FS249.

Christensen, Lawrence O., William E. Foley, and Gary Kremer, eds. *Dictionary of Missouri Biography*. Columbia, MO: University of Missouri Press, 1999.

Christians, Clifford G., John P. Ferre, and P. Mark Fackler. *Good News: Social Ethics and the Press*. New York: Oxford University Press, 1993.

Christians, Clifford. "Enforcing Media Codes." *Journal of Mass Media Ethics* 1, no. 1 (Fall/Winter 1985-6): 14-21.

Claypoole, Ted, and Theresa Payton. *Protecting Your Internet Identity: Are You Naked Online?* Rowman & Littlefield, 2016.

Clayton, Charles C. *Sigma Delta Chi: Fifty Years of Freedom*. Carbondale, IL: Southern Illinois University Press, 1959, 43.

Cockburn, Harry. "China Blacklists Millions of People from Booking Flights as Social Credit System Introduced." *Independent*. November 23, 2018. https://www.independent.co.uk/news/world/asia/china-social-credit-system-flight-booking-blacklisted-beijing-points-a8646316.html.

Copeland, David A. The *Antebellum Era: Primary Documents on Events from 1820 to 1860*. Westport, CT: Greenwood Publishing Group, 2003.

Commission on Freedom of the Press. *A Free and Responsible Press: A General Report on Mass Communication, Newspapers, Radio, Motion*

*Pictures, Magazines, and Books.* Chicago: University of Chicago Press, 1947.

Conboy, Martin. *Journalism Studies: The Basics.* New York: Routledge, 2013.

Concha, Joe. "Presidential Race Coverage Focusing Solely on Sensationalism." The Hill.com. August 3, 2016. https://thehill.com/blogs/pundits-blog/presidential-campaign/290228-presidential-race-coverage-focusing-solely-on.

Conlin, Joseph R. *The American Past: A Survey of American History, Since 1865.* Vol. 2. Boston: Wadsworth, 2010.

Cookman, Claude Hubert. *American Photojournalism: Motivations and Meanings.* Evanston, IL: Northwestern University Press, 2009.

Cook, Fred J. *The Muckrakers: Crusading Journalists Who Changed America.* Garden City, NY: Doubleday, 1972.

Cooper, Kent. *Barriers Down: The Story of the News Agency Epoch.* Port Washington, NY: Kennikat Press, 1942.

Cramp, Arthur Joseph. *"Patent Medicines" The Nostrum and the Public Health: Truth in Advertising Drug Products.* American Medical Association Bureau of Investigation, Chicago: 1923.

Crouse, Timothy. *The Boys on the Bus.* New York: Random House, 2003.

Crouthamel, James L. *Bennett's New York Herald and the Rise of the Popular Press.* Syracuse, NY: Syracuse University Press, 1989.

Curry, James A., Richard B. Riley, and Richard M. Battistoni. *Constitutional Government: The American Experience.* Dubuque, IA: Kendall Hunt Publishing, 2003.

Cwalina, Wojciech, Andrzej Falkowski, and Bruce I. Newman. *Political Marketing: Theoretical and Strategic Foundations.* Philadelphia: Routledge, 2015.

Davis, Elmer Holmes. *History of the New York Times, 1851-1921.* New York: Press of J. J. Little & Ives, Co., 1921.

Davis, Michael, and Andrew Stark. *Conflict of Interest in the Professions.* New York: Oxford University Press, 2001.

Davison, Alastair. *From Subject to Citizen: Australian Citizenship in the Twentieth Century.* New York: Cambridge University Press, 1997.

Denis, Brian. *Pulitzer: A Life.* Hoboken, NJ: A Life John Wiley & Sons, Inc., 2001.

Dewy, Caitlin. "Google Maps' White House Glitch, Flickr Auto-Tag, and the Case of the Racist Algorithm." *Washington Post.* May 20, 2015. https://www.washingtonpost.com/news/the-intersect/wp/2015/05/20/google-maps-white-houseglitch-flickr-auto-tag-and-the-case-of-the-racist-algorithm/.

Dicken-Garcia, Hazel. *Journalistic Standards in Nineteenth Century America.* Madison, WI: University of Wisconsin Press, 1989.

Dickinson, Henry Winram. *A Short History of the Steam Engine.* Cambridge, UK: Cambridge University Press, 1939.

DiGirolamo, Vincent. *Crying the News: A History of America's Newsboys.* New York: Oxford University Press, 2019.

Dillon, Matthew, and Lynda Garland. *Ancient Greece: Social and Historical Documents from Archaic Times to the Death of Socrates.* New York: Routledge, 2000.

Dingwall, Robert, and Philip Lewis. *The Sociology the Professions: Lawyers, Doctors and Others.* New York: St. Martin's Press, 1983.

*Doings of the Editors & Publishers' Association of Maine at Biddleford, August 7 & 8, 1867.* Portland, ME: Thurston & Co., 1867.

Donaldson, Sam. *Hold On, Mr. President.* New York: Fawcett Crest, 1987.

Douglas, George H. *The Golden Age of Newspapers.* Westport, CT: Greenwood Press, 1934.

Dublin, Thomas. *Women at Work: The Transformation of Work and Community in Lowell, Massachusetts, 1826-1860.* New York City: Columbia University Press, 1979.

Duffy, Margaret, and Esther Thorson. *Persuasion Ethics Today*. New York: Routledge, 2015.

Durkheim, Emile. *The Division of Labor in Society.* London: The Macmillan Company, 1933.

Dvorkin, Jeffrey. "Why Click-Bait Will be the Death of Journalism." PBS. April 27, 2018. https://www.pbs.org/newshour/economy/what-you-dont-know-about-click-bait-journalism-could-kill-you.

Elliott, Philip. *The Sociology of the Professions.* New York: Herder and Herder, 1973.

Elliott, Stuart. "Liquor Industry Ends Its Ad Ban in Broadcasting." *New York Times*. November 8, 1996. https://www.nytimes.com/1996/11/08/business/liquor-industry-ends-its-ad-ban-in-broadcasting.html.

Emery, Edwin, and Michael Emery. *The Press and America: An Interpretive History of the Mass Media.* Upper Saddle River, NJ: Prentice Hall, 1984.

Entman, Robert M. *Democracy without Citizens: Media and the Decay of American Politics.* New York: Oxford University Press, 1990.

Entman, Robert M. "Framing: Toward Clarification of a Fractured Paradigm." *Journal of Communication* 43, no. 4 (Autumn 1993), 51-58.

Erickson, Emily. "Yellow Journalism." In *Encyclopedia of American Journalism,* edited by Stephen L. Vaughn, 607-8. New York: Routledge, 2008.

Erler, Edward J. "The Great Fence to Liberty." In *Liberty, Property and the Foundations of the American Constitution.* edited by Ellen Frankel Paul and Howard Dickman, 43-63. New York: State University of New York Press, 1989.

Ezra, Ovadia. *Moral Dilemmas in Real Life: Current Issues in Applied Ethics.* Berlin, Germany: Springer Science and Business Media, 2006.

Fahs, Chad. *How to Do Everything with YouTube.* New York: McGraw Hill Professional, 2007.

Farhi, Paul. "Sarah Sanders Promotes an Altered Video of CNN Reporter, Sparking Allegations of Visual Propaganda." *Washington Post.* November 8, 2018. https://www.washingtonpost.com/lifestyle/style/sarah-sanders-promotes-an-altered-video-of-cnn-reporter-sparking-allegations-of-visual-propaganda/2018/11/08/33210126-e375-11e8-b759-3d88a5ce9e19_story.html?utm_term=.5c51bf3a8412.

Farrar, Ronald T. *A Creed for My Profession: Walter Williams, Journalist to the World.* Columbia, MO: University of Missouri Press, 1998.

Feinberg, Joel. *The Moral Limits of Criminal Law: Offense to Others.* New York: Oxford University Press, 1985.

Flaherty, David H., *Protecting Privacy in Surveillance Societies: The Federal Republic of Germany, Sweden, France, Canada, and the United States.* Chapel Hill, NC: University of North Carolina Press, 2014.

Ford, Edwin, and Edwin Emery. *Highlights in the History of the American Press: A Book of Readings.* Minneapolis, MN: University of Minnesota Press, 1954.

Foreman, Gene. *The Ethical Journalist: Making Responsible Decisions in the Digital Age.* Malden, MA: John Wiley & Sons, Inc., 2015.

Foust, Jim. *Online Journalism: Principles and Practices of News on the Web.* 3rd ed. New York: Routledge, 2017.

Fowler, Geoffrey A. "I Fell for Facebook Fake News. Here's Why Millions of You Did, Too." *Washington Post.* October 18, 2018. https://www.washingtonpost.com/technology/2018/10/18/i-fell-facebook-fake-news-heres-why-millions-you-did-too/?utm_term=.bd3e078762a1.

Franklin, Bob, and Mark Hanna. "Advertising." In *Key Concepts in Journalism Studies*, edited by Bob Franklin, Martin Hamer, Hark Hanna, Marie Kinsey, and John E. Richardson, 8-10. Thousand Oaks, CA: Sage, 2005.

Friedman, Andrea. *Prurient Interests: Gender, Democracy, and Obscenity in New York City, 1909-1945.* New York: Columbia University Press, 2000.

Gans, Herbert J. *Deciding What's News: A Study of the CBS Evening News, NBC Nightly News, Newsweek, and Time.* Evanston, IL: Northwestern University Press, 2004.

Garsd, Jasmine. "Internet Memes and 'The Right to be Forgotten.'" *NPR.* March 3, 2015. https://www.npr.org/sections/alltechconsidered/2015/03/03/390463119 /internet-memes-and-the-right-to-be-forgotten.

Gilligan, Eileen N. *Competing for News: Reporter's Use of Competition and Cooperation in the Production of News.* Madison, WI: University of Wisconsin Press, 2004.

Glenn, William Meharry. *The Sigma Delta Chi Story: 1909-1949.* Coral Gables, FL: Glade House, 1949.

Goffman, Erving. *Frame Analysis: An Essay on the Organization of Experience.* New York: Harper & Row, 1974.

Goodman, Matthew. *The Sun and the Moon.* New York: Basic Books, 2008.

Greeley, Arthur Philip. *The Food and Drugs Act, June 30, 1906.* Washington, DC: John Byrne and Company, 1907.

Green, Norma, Stephen Lacy, and Jean Folkerts. "Chicago Journalists at the Turn of the Century: Bohemians All?" *Journalism Quarterly* 66 (Winter 1989): 813-821.

Grote, George. *History of Greece.* London: John Murray, 1851.

Grove, Lloyd, Mike Giglio, Dan Ephron, and William Underhill. "Rupert's Red Menace." *Newsweek.* July 25, 2011, 40-44.

Grynbaum, Michael M., Scott Shane and Emily Flitter. "How an Affair Between a Security Aide Has Rattled Washington Media." *New York Times.* June 24, 2018. https://www.nytimes.com/2018/06/24/business/media/james-wolfe-ali-watkins-leaks-reporter.html.

Hardt, Hanno. "Reinventing the Press in the Age of Commercial Appeals: Writings on and about Public Journalism." In *The Idea of Public Journalism* edited by Theodore Lewis Glasser, 197-209. New York: Guilford Press, 1999.

Helmus, Todd C., Elizabeth Bodine-Baron, Andrew Radin, Madeline Magnuson, Joshua Mendelsohn, William Marcellino, Andriy Bega, and Zev Winkelman. *Russian Social Media Influence: Understanding Russian Propaganda in Eastern Europe.* N. p.: Rand Corporation, 2018.

Herman, John. "Self-Correcting Beyond a Web Era Marked by Sensationalism." *New York Times.* March 20, 2016. https://www.nytimes.com/2016/03/21/business/media/self-correcting-beyond-a-web-era-of-sensationalism.html.

Hermida, Alfred. "Twittering the News: The Emergence of Ambient Journalism." *Journalism Practice* 4, no. 3 (July 2010): 297-308.

Hirst, Martin. *Navigating Social Journalism: A Handbook for Media Literacy and Citizen Journalism.* New York: Routledge, 2019.

Hitchens, Lesley. *Broadcasting Pluralism and Diversity: A Comparative Study of Policy and Regulation.* Portland, OR: Hart Publishing, 2006.

Hofstadtler, Richard. *The Age of Reform: From Bryan to F.D.R.* New York: Vintage Books, 2011.

Holbrook, Stewart. *The Golden Age of Quackery.* New York: Collier Books, 1959.

Holt, Jennifer. *Empires of Entertainment: Media Industries and the Politics of Deregulation, 1980-1996.* New Brunswick, NJ: Rutgers University Press, 2011.

Hudson, Frederic. *Journalism in the United States: From 1690 to 1872.* New York: Harper and Brothers Publishers, 1873.

Hughes, Everett Cherrington. *Men and Their Work.* Glencoe, IL: The Free Press, 1958.

Ibish, Hussein. "Why America Turned Off Al Jazeera." *New York Times.* February 17, 2016. https://www.nytimes.com/2016/02/18/opinion/why-america-turned-off-al-jazeera.html.

"Incidents in Foreign Graphic Circles." *The Inland Printer.* Vol. 54. Chicago: The Inland Printer Company Publishers, 1915.

Isaac, Mike. "Mark Zuckerberg's Call to Regulate Facebook, Explained." *New York Times.* March 30, 2019. https://www.nytimes.com/2019/03/30/technology/mark-zuckerberg-facebook-regulation-explained.html.

Jamison, Kathleen Hall. *Cyber War: How Russian Hackers and Trolls Helped Elect a President: What We Don't, Can't, and Do Know.* New York: Oxford University Press, 2018.

Janik, Erika. *Marketplace of the Marvelous: The Strange Origins of Modern Medicine.* Boston: Beacon Press, 2014.

Jensen, Elizabeth. "When is a Friendship a Conflict of Interest?" *NPR.* February 26, 2016. https://www.npr.org/sections/ombudsman/2016/02/26/467813499/when-is-a-friendship-a-conflict-of-interest.

Jensen, Ric. "Blogola, Sponsored Posts, and the Ethics of Blogging." In *The Ethics of Emerging Media*, edited by Bruce E. Drushel and Kathleen German, 213-234. New York: The Continuum International Publishing Group, 2011.

Jervis, John. *Sensational Subjects: The Dramatization of Experience in the Modern World.* New York: Bloomsbury Academic, 2015.

Jones, Meg Leta. *Ctrl + Z: The Right to be Forgotten.* New York: New York University Press, 2018.

Kalb, Marvin. *The Enemy of the People: Trump's War on the Press, The New McCarthyism, and the Threat to American Democracy.* Washington, DC: The Brookings Institution, 2018.

Kang, Cecilia, David Streitfeld, and Annie Karni. "Antitrust Troubles Snowball for Tech Giants as Lawmakers Join In." *New York Times.* June 3, 2019. https://www.nytimes.com/2019/06/03/technology/facebook-ftc-antitrust.html.

Kaul, Arthur J. "The Proletarian Journalist: A Critique of Professionalization." *Journal of Mass Media Ethics* 1, no. 2 (Spring/Summer 1986): 47-55.

Keith, Susan. "Scandal at the Top in TV News." In *Scandal in a Digital Age*, edited by Hinda Mandell and Gina Masullo Chen, 161-172. New York: Palgrave Macmillan, 2016.

Kennedy, III, Samuel V. *Samuel Hopkins Adams and the Business of Writing.* Syracuse, NY: Syracuse University Press, 1999.

King, Dan. *Quackery Unmasked.* New York: D. Clapp, 1858.

Kitay, William. *The Challenge of Medicine.* New York: Holt, Rinehart and Winston, 1963.

Knightly, Philip. *The First Casualty.* New York: Harcourt, Brace, Jovanovich, 1975.

Kobre, Sidney. *Development of American Journalism.* Dubuque, IA: Wm. C. Brown Company Publishers, 1969.

Kobre, Sidney. *The Yellow Press and Gilded Age Journalism.* Gainesville, FL: Florida State University, 1964.

Konieczna, Magda. *Journalism Without Profit: Making News when the Market Fails.* New York: Oxford University Press, 2018.

Kovach, Bill, and Tom Rosenstiel. *The Elements of Journalism: What News People Should Know and Public Should Expect.* New York: Three Rivers Press, 2001.

Kusch, Larry. "Pallister Questions Long-Term Value of Ottawa's Media-Subsidy Plan." *Winnipeg Free Press.* November 23, 2018. https://www.winnipegfreepress.com/local/pallister-questions-long-term-value-of-ottawas-media-subsidy-plan-501147331.html.

Kuypers, Jim A. *Partisan Journalism: A History of Media Bias in the United States.* New York: Rowman & Littlefield Publishers, 2013.

Lambeth, Edward B. *Committed Journalism.* 2nd ed. Indianapolis, IN: Indiana University Press, 1992.

Landes, David S. *The Unbound Prometheus.* Cambridge, UK: Press Syndicate of the University of Cambridge, 1969.

Larson, Magali Sarfatti. *The Rise of Professionalism: A Sociological*

*Analysis.* Berkeley, CA: University of California Press, 1977.

Latham, Robert Gordon. *Samuel Johnson's A Dictionary of the English Language.* London: Longmans, Green, & Co., 1876.

Lawson, Linda. *Truth in Publishing: Federal Regulation of the Press's Business Practices.* Carbondale, IL: Southern Illinois University Press, 1993.

Lee, Alfred McClung. *The Daily Newspaper in America.* New York: Macmillan Company, 1937.

Lee, James Melvin. *History of American Journalism.* New York: Garden City Publishing Co., Inc., 1923.

Lee, William, Daxton R. Stewart and Johnathan Peters. *The Law of Public Communication.* New York: Routledge, 2017.

Leonhardt, David. "A French Lesson for the American Media." *New York Times.* May 9, 2017. https://www.nytimes.com/2017/05/09/opinion/a-french-lesson-for-the-american-media.html.

Leibovich, Louis. *Richard Nixon, Watergate and the Press: A Historical Perspective.* Westport, CT: Greenwood Publishing Group, 2003.

Levmore, Saul. "The Internet's Anonymity Problem." In *The Offensive Internet: Speech, Privacy and Reputation,* edited by Saul Levmore and Martha Nussbaum, 50-67. Cambridge, MA: Harvard University Press, 2010.

Levy, Leonard W. *Origin of the Bill of Rights.* New Haven, CT: Yale University Press.

Lindert, Peter H. *Growing Public: Social Spending and Economic Growth Since the Eighteenth Century.* New York: Cambridge University Press, 2006.

Lindsey, Robert. "Carol Burnett Given $1.6 Million in Suit Against National Enquirer." *New York Times.* March 27, 1981. https://www.nytimes.com/1981/03/27/us/carol-burnett-given-1.6-million-in-suit-against-national-enquirer.html.

Lippmann, Walter. *Public Opinion.* New York: Harcourt, Brace and Company, Inc., 1922.

Lipschultz, Jeremy. *Broadcast and Internet Indecency: Defining Free Speech.* New York: Routledge, 2008.

Loeb, Thom. *Editing for the Digital Age.* Thousand Oaks, CA: CQ Press 2016.

Lucas, Jr., Robert E. *Lectures on Economic Growth.* Cambridge, MA: Harvard University Press, 2002.

Maihafer, Harry James. *The General and the Journalists: Ulysses S. Grant, Horace Greeley and Charles Dana.* McLean, VA: Brassey's Inc., 1998.

Marc, David. *Demographic Vistas: Television in American Culture.* Philadelphia: University of Pennsylvania Press, 1996.

Marmaduke, John. "May 27, 1872 Annual Missouri Press Association Address." In J. W. Barrett, ed. *History and Transactions of the Editors and Publishers Association of Missouri.* Canton, MO: Canton Press Print, 1876.

Marzolf, Marion Tuttle. *Civilizing Voices: American Press Criticism 1880-1950.* New York: Longman Publishing Group, 1991.

Mathewson, Joe. *Law and Ethics for Today's Journalist.* New York: Routledge, 2015.

Maverick, Augustus. *Henry D. Raymond and the New York Press for Thirty Years: Progress of American Journalism from 1840 To 1870.* Hartford, CT: A. S. Hale and Company, 1870.

McChesney, Robert D. *The Problem of the Media: U.S. Communication Politics in the Twenty-First Century.* New York: New York University Press, 2004.

McChesney, Robert W., and Victor Pickard. *Will the Last Reporter Please Turn Out the Lights: The Collapse of Journalism and What Can be Done to Fix It.* New York: The New Press, 2011.

McPhaul, John J. *Deadlines and Monkeyshines: The Fabled World of Chicago Journalists.* Englewood Cliffs, NJ: Prentice-Hall, 1962.

McQuail, Denis. *McQuail's Mass Communication Theory.* Thousand Oaks, CA: Sage, 2005.

McStay, Andrew. *Privacy and the Media.* Los Angeles: Sage Publications, 2017.

Medoff, Norman J., and Barbara Kaye. *Electronic Media, Then, Now, and Later.* Abingdon, UK: Taylor & Francis, 2013.

Meggs, Philip B. *A History of Graphic Design.* Hoboken, NJ: John Wiley & Sons, Inc., 1998.

Meraz, Sharon, and Zizi Papacharissi. "Networked Framing and Gatekeeping." In *The Sage Handbook of Digital Journalism,* edited by Tamara Witschge, C.W. Anderson, David Domingo, and Alfred Hermida, 95-114. Thousand Oaks, CA: Sage, 2016.

Merrill, John C. *The Dialectic in Journalism: Toward a Responsible Use of Press Freedom.* Baton Rouge, LA: Louisiana State University Press, 1993.

Merrill, John C. *The Imperative of Freedom: A Philosophy of Journalistic Autonomy.* New York: Hastings House Publishers, 1974.

Merrill, John C. "Journalistic Professionalization: Danger to Freedom and Pluralism," *Journal of Mass Media Ethics* 1, no. 2 (Spring/Summer 1986): 56-60.

*Michigan Press Association at the Sixteenth Annual Meeting Held at Detroit, March 29-30, 1883.* Nashville, MI: News Steam Print, 1883.

Milton, John. *Areopagitica: A Speech of Mr. John Milton for the Liberty of Unlicenc'd Printing, to the Parliament of England.* London: n.p., 1644.

Mindich, David T. Z. *The Mediated World: A New Approach to Mass Communication and Culture.* Lanham, MD: Rowman and Littlefield, 2019.

Moore, Adam D. *Privacy Rights: Moral and Legal Foundations.* University Park, PA: Penn State Press, 2010.

Moore, John Weeks. *Historical Notes on Printers and Printing 1420 To 1886.* Concord, MA: Republican Press Association, 1886.

Moore, Wilbert E. *The Professions: Roles and Rules.* New York: Russell Sage Foundation, 1970.

Moran, James. *Printing Presses: History and Development from the Fifteenth Century to Modern Times.* Los Angeles: University of California Press, 1978.

Morris, James McGrath. "William Randolph Hearst." In *Encyclopedia of American Journalism*, edited by Stephen L. Vaughn, 211-12. New York: Routledge, 2008.

Mott, Frank Luther. *American Journalism: A History of Newspapers in the United States Through 250 Years 1690 to 1940.* New York: Macmillan Company, 1945.

Mussell, James. "The Foundation and Early Years of the News of the World: 'Capacious Double Sheets.'" In *The News of the World and the British Press, 1843-2011*, edited by Laurel Brake, Chandrika Kaul and Mark W. Turner, 11-26. New York: Palgrave Macmillan, 2016.

Musson, Albert Edward, and Eric Robinson. *Science and Technology in the Industrial Revolution.* Milton Park, UK: Taylor & Francis, 1989.

Nasaw, David. *The Chief: The Life of William Randolph Hearst.* New York: Houghton Mifflin, 2000.

"News of the World: 1843-2011." *The Press Gazette*. July 8, 2011. www.pressgazette.co.uk/node/4758.

"The News of the World's Sensational History." *The Guardian*. July 7, 2011. www.guardian.co.uk/media/2011/jul/07/news-of-the-world-history.

"News Use Across Social Media Platforms 2017." *Pew Research Center*. August 23, 2017. http://www.journalism.org/2017/09/07/news-use-across-social-media-platforms-2017/pi_17-08-23_socialmediaupdate_0-01/.

Noam, Eli M. *Media Ownership and Concentration in America.* New York: Oxford University Press, 2009.

Nobile, Philip. "The Pulitzer Surprise: The Washington Post's 'Jimmygate.'" *New York Magazine*. April 27, 2020.

Olasky, Marvin. *Central Ideas in the Development of American Journalism: A Narrative History*. New York: Routledge, 2016.

Ovadya, Aviv. "What is Credibility Made of." *Columbia Journalism Review*. March 21, 2019. https://www.cjr.org/tow_center_reports/ovadya-credibility-journalism-ocasio.php.

Owen, Howard. "Advertising Rates and Agencies." In *Transactions of the Maine Editors and Publishers' Association, from 1870 To 1874, Inclusive,* edited by Joseph Wood. Wiscasset. ME: Printed by Joseph Wood, 1874.

Patching, Roger, and Martin Hirst. *Journalism Ethics: Arguments and Cases for the Twenty-first Century*. New York: Routledge, 2014.

"Patent Medicines," *U. S. House Journal,* House Report No. 52, 30th Cong., 1849, 31.

Papacharissi, Zizi. *Affective Publics: Sentiment, Technology, and Politics*. New York: Oxford University Press, 2015.

Pavlik, John V. *Journalism and the New Media*. New York: Columbia University Press, 2001.

Payne, George. *History of Journalism in the United States*. New York: D. Appleton-Century Company, Incorporated, 1940.

Perry, James M. *A Bohemian Brigade, the Civil War Correspondents: Mostly Rough—Sometimes Ready*. Hoboken, NJ: Wiley, 2000.

Phillips, Whitney. *This is Why We Can't Have Nice Things: Mapping the Relationship Between Online Trolling and Mainstream Culture*. Cambridge, MA: MIT Press, 2015.

Pickard, Victor. *Democracy without Journalism? Confronting the Misinformation Society*. New York: Oxford University Press, 2019.

Pins, Alice Fox. *Read All About It: 50 Years of ASNE*. N. p.: American Society of Newspaper Editors, 1974.

Pizzitola, Louis. *Hearst Over Hollywood: Power, Passion, and Propaganda in the Movies*. New York: Columbia University Press, 2002.

Posner, Eric. "We All Have the Right to be Forgotten." *Slate*. May 14, 2014. https://slate.com/news-and-politics/2014/05/the-european-right-to-be-forgotten-is-just-what-the-internet-needs.html.

Power-Berrey, Robert J. *The Romance of a Great Newspaper*. London: News of the World, 1932.

Pratte, Paul Alfred. *Gods Within the Machine: A History of the American Society of Newspaper Editors, 1923-1993*. Westport, CT: Praeger, 1995.

Pray, Isaac Clarke. *Memoirs of James Gordon Bennet and His Times*. New

York: Stringer & Townsend, 1855.

*Press Club of Chicago: Official Reference Book of the Press Club of Chicago Oldest Press Club in the World.* Chicago: Press Club of Chicago, 1922.

Prior, Markus. *Post Broadcast Democracy: How Media Choice Increases Media Inequality.* New York: Cambridge University Press, 2007.

Procter, Ben. *William Randolph Hearst: The Early Years, 1863-1910.* New York: Oxford University Press, 1998.

"Propaganda for Reform," *Journal of the American Medical Association* 67, no. 4 (1916): 1774.

Quinn, Aaron. *Virtue Ethics and Professional Journalism.* New York: Springer Publishing, 2018.

Quinn, Stephen, and Stephen Lamble. *Online Newsgathering: Research and Reporting for Journalism.* Burlington, MA: Focal Press, 2012.

Reader, W. J. *Professional Men.* London: Weidenfeld and Nicholson, 1966.

Robinson, Harriet H. *Loom and Spindle, or Life Among the Early Mill Girls.* New York: Thomas Y. Crowell & Company, 1898.

Roll, Erich. *An Early Experiment in Industrial Organisation, being a History of the Firm of Boulton & Watt, 1775-1805.* New York: Longmans, Green and Co., 1930.

Rosen, William. *The Most Powerful Idea in the World: A Story of Steam, Industry and Invention.* Chicago: University of Chicago Press, 2012.

Rosenberg, Charles E., and William H. Helfand. *"Every Man his Own Doctor" Popular Medicine in Early America.* Philadelphia: Library Company of Philadelphia, 1998.

Rusbridger, Alan. "How We Broke the Murdoch Scandal." *Newsweek.* July 25, 2011, 45-47.

Rutenberg, Jim. "Buzzfeed News in Limbo Land." *New York Times.* January 20, 2019. https://www.nytimes.com/2019/01/20/business/media/buzzfeed-trump-mueller-backlash.html.

Saalberg, Harvey. "The Canons of Journalism: A 50 Year Perspective." *Journalism Quarterly* 5, no. 4 (1973): 731-734.

Sachsman, David B., and David W. Bulla, eds., *Sensationalism: Murder, Mayhem, Mudslinging, Scandals, and Disasters in 19th Century Reporting.* Piscataway, NJ: Transaction Publishers, 2013.

Sambrook, Richard. "Objectivity and Impartiality in Digital News Coverage." *The Guardian.* June 12, 2014. https://www.theguardian.com/media/media-blog/2014/jun/12/objectivity-and-impartiality-in-digital-news-coverage.

Savage, William. *A Dictionary of the Art of Printing.* London: Longman, Brown, Green, and Longmans, 1841.

Savory, Thomas. *The Miner's Friend, or an Engine to Raise Water by Fire, Described by Captain Thomas Savery.* London: J. McCormick, 62, Paternoster Row, 1829.

Saxonhouse, Arlene W. *Free Speech and Democracy in Ancient Athens.* New York: Cambridge University Press, 2006.

Scharf, John Thomas. *History of Saint Louis City and County: From the Earliest Periods to the Present Day.* Philadelphia: L. H. Everts, 1883.

Schroder, Kim Christian. "The Best of Both Worlds." In *Rethinking the Media Audience: The New Agenda,* edited by Pertti Alasuutari, 38-68. Thousand Oaks, CA: Sage, 1999.

Schudson, Michael. *Discovering the News: A Social History of American Newspapers.* New York: Basic Books, 1981.

Schudson, Michael. *The Power of News.* Cambridge, MA: Harvard University Press, 1995.

Schwartz, Oscar. "You Thought Fake News Was Bad? Deep Fakes Are Where Truth Goes to Die." *The Guardian.* November 12, 2018. https://www.theguardian.com/technology/2018/nov/12/deep-fakes-fake-news-truth.

Seidel, Marc-David L. "Factors Impacting Click-Through Rate." In *Encyclopedia of Social Media and Politics*, edited by Kerrick Harvey, 281. Thousand Oaks, CA: Sage Publications, 2014.

Sernoffsky, Evan. "Five Firefighters among Dozen-plus Patients Burned in Camp Fire." *San Francisco Chronicle.* November 15, 2018. https://www.sfchronicle.com/california-wildfires/amp/Five-firefighters-among-dozen-plus-patients-13396604.php.

Shane, Scott. "The Fake Americans Russia Created to Influence the Election." *New York Times.* September 7, 2017. https://www.nytimes.com/2017/09/07/us/politics/russia-facebook-twitter-election.html.

Shaw, Ronald E. *Canals for a Nation: The Canal Era in the United States, 1790-1860.* Lexington, KY: University of Kentucky, 2014.

Sherman, Gabriel. *The Loudest Voice in the Room: How the Brilliant, Bombastic, Roger Ailes Built Fox News and Divided a Country.* New York: Random House Publishing, 2013.

Shiller, Robert J. *Narrative Economics: How Stories Go Viral and Drive Major Economic Events.* Princeton, NJ: Princeton University Press, 2019.

Shoemaker, Floyd Calvin. *Missouri and Missourians: Land of Contrast and People of Achievement,* 2 vols. Chicago: Lewis Publishing Company,

1943.

Shoemaker, Pamela J., and Timothy Vos. *Gatekeeping Theory.* New York: Routledge, 2009.

Shoemaker, Pamela J., and Stephen D. Reese. *Mediating the Message: Theories of Influences of Mass Media Content.* White Plains, NY: Longman, 1995.

Shoemaker, Pamela. "A New Gatekeeping Model." In *Social Meanings of News*, edited by Daniel A. Berkowitz, 57-62. Thousand Oaks, CA: Sage, 1997.

Shoot, Brittany. "Watch: Julie Chen Quits 'The Talk' Via Video Following the Resignation of Former CBS CEO Les Moonves." *Fortune.* September 18, 2018. http://fortune.com/2018/09/18/watch-julie-chen-quit-the-talk-video-moonves/.

Siebert, Fred S., Theodore Peterson, and Wilbert Schramm. *Four Theories of the Press.* Urbana, IL: University of Illinois Press, 1963.

Simmons, Steven J. *The Fairness Doctrine and the Media.* Berkeley, CA: University of California Press, 1978.

Simon, Paul. *Freedom's Champion: Elijah Lovejoy.* Carbondale, IL: Southern Illinois University Press, 1994.

Simonds, Christopher. *Samuel Slater's Mill and the Industrial Revolution.* Englewood Cliffs, NJ: Silver Burdett Press, 1990.

Sinclair, Upton. *The Brass Check.* Pasadena, CA: Self, 1919.

Sinclair, Upton. *The Jungle.* New York: Doubleday, Page & Company, 1906.

Singer, Dorothy G., and Jerome L. Singer. *Handbook of Children and the Media.* Thousand Oaks, CA: Sage, 2001.

Sloan, William David. *Makers of the Media Mind: Journalism Educators and Their Ideas.* New York: Routledge, 2014.

Smith, Adam. *An Inquiry into the Nature and Causes of the Wealth of Nations.* London: W. Strahan, 1776.

Smith, David. "Why does Trump Hate Jeff Bezos: Is it About Power or Money?" *The Guardian.* June 17, 2018. https://www.theguardian.com/technology/2018/jun/17/donald-trump-jeff-bezos-amazon-washington-post-power-money.

Smith, Jeffery A. *War and Press Freedom: The Problem of Prerogative Power.* New York: The Oxford University Press, 1999.

Smith, Ron F. *Ethics in Journalism.* 6th ed. Malden, MA: Blackwell Publishing, 2008.

Southward, John. *Practical Printing: A Handbook of the Art of Typography.* London: J. M. Powell & Son, 1884.

Spencer, David R. *The Yellow Journalism: The Press and America's Emergence as a World Power.* Evanston, IL: Northwestern University Press, 2007.

Stage, Sarah. *Female Complaints: Lydia Pinkham and the Business of Women's Medicine.* New York: W. W. Norton and Co., 1979.

Starr, Paul. *The Social Transformation of American Medicine: The Rise of a Solemn Profession and the Making of a Vast Industry.* New York: Basic Books, 1982.

Stanhope, Ghita, and George Peabody Gooch. *The Life of Charles, Third Earl of Stanhope.* London: Longmans, Green and Company, 1914.

Stearns, Peter N. *The Industrial Revolution in World History.* Boulder, CO: Westview Press, 1998.

Stephens, Mitchell. *Beyond the News: The Future of Journalism.* New York: Columbia University Press, 2014.

Stevens, John D. *Sensationalism and the New York Press.* New York: Columbia University Press, 1991.

Stone, Gerald C., Mary K. O'Donnell, and Stephen Banning. "Public Perceptions of Newspaper's Watchdog Role." *Newspaper Research Journal* 18, no. 1-2 (January 1997): 86-102.

Swanberg, W. A. *Pulitzer.* New York: Charles Scribner's Sons, 1967.

Sutcliffe, Alice Clary. *Robert Fulton and the "Clermont".* New York: The Century Company, 1909.

Taylor, John. *Body Horror: Photojournalism, Catastrophe and War.* Manchester, UK: Manchester University Press, 1998.

Thomson, Byerly H. *The Choice of a Profession.* London: n. p., 1857.

Thomson, Ross. *Structures of Change in the Mechanical Age: Technological Invention in the United States 1790-1865.* Baltimore, MD: The Johns Hopkins University Press, 2009.

Tidskr, Sven Med. "From Barber to Surgeon: The Process of Professionalization." *Svensk Medicinhistorisk Tidskrift* 11, no. 1 (2007): 69-87.

Timbs, John. *Doctors and Patients,* 2 vols. London: R. Bentley and Son, 1873.

Trager, Robert, Susan Dente Ross, and Amy Reynolds. *The Law of Journalism and Mass Communication.* 6th ed. Thousand Oaks, CA: CQ Press, 2018.

*Transactions of the Editors and Publishers' Association of Maine.* Portland, ME: Monitor Printing Company, 1869.

Tremayne, Mark. "Harnessing the Active Audience: Synthesizing Blog Research and Lessons for the Future of Media." In *Blogging, Citizenship, and the Future of Media*, edited by Mark Tremayne, 261-72. New York: Routledge, 2012.

Tuchman, Gaye. *Making News: A Study in the Construction of Reality.* New York: Free Press, 1978.

Tversky, Amos, and Daniel Kahneman. "Judgment Under Uncertainty, Heuristics and Biases." *Science* 185, no. 4157 (September 1974), 1124-1131.

Utley, Garrick. *Live from the Trenches: The Changing Role of Television News.* Carbondale, IL: University of Southern Illinois Press, 1998.

Velasco, Jesus. *American Presidential Elections in a Comparative Perspective: The World is Watching.* Lanham, MD: Rowman and Littlefield, 2019.

Vollmer, Howard M., and Donald L. Mills. *Professionalization.* Englewood Cliffs, NJ: Prentice-Hall Inc., 1966.

Vos, Timothy, and François Heinderyckx. *Gatekeeping in Transition.* New York: Routledge, 2015.

Wadhwa, Kush, and Rowena Rodrigues. "Evaluating Privacy Impact Assessments." In *Privacy and Security in the Digital Age: Privacy in the Age of Super-Technologies*, eds. Michael Friedewald and Ronald J. Pohoryles, 161-180. New York: Routledge, 2016.

Wakefield, Robert I., and Coleman F. Barney. "Communication in an Unfettered Marketplace: Ethical Interrelations of Business, Government, and Stakeholders." *Journal of Mass Media Ethics* 16, no. 2 & 3 (2001): 213-233.

Wahl-Jogensen, Karin, and Thomas Hanitzsch. *The Handbook of Journalism Studies.* Philadelphia, PA: Routledge, 2009.

Waisbord, Silvio. *Reinventing Professionalism: Journalism and News in Global Perspective.* Malden, MA: Polity Press, 2013.

Ward, Stephen J. A. *The Invention of Journalism Ethics: The Path to Objectivity and Beyond.* 2nd ed. Chicago: McGill-Queen's University Press, 2015.

Warren, Samuel, and Louis Brandeis. "The Right to Privacy." *Harvard Law Review* 193, no. 4. December 15, 1890.

Webb, W. L. *Battles and Biographies of Missourians or the Civil War Period of Our State.* 2 vols. 2nd ed. Kansas City, MO: Hudson-Kimberly Publishing Company, 1903.

Whetmore, Edward J. *Mediamerica: Form, Content and Consequence of Mass Communication.* Belmont, CA: Wadsworth Publishing Company, 1982.

Wike, Victoria S. *Kant on Happiness in Ethics.* Albany, NY: State University of New York Press, 1994.

Wile, Rob. "Mark Zuckerberg Has Made More Money Than Anyone Else in 2017—Even Jeff Bezos." *Money.* August 8, 2017. http://time.com/money/4891103/mark-zuckerberg-jeff-bezos-billionaires-net.-worth-2017/.

Will, George. "George Bush: The Sound of a Lapdog." *Washington Post.* Jan. 30, 1986.

Wilkie, Franc Bangs. *Personal Reminiscences of Thirty-five Years of Journalism.* Chicago: F. J. Schulte & Company, 1891.

Wilkinson, Todd. *Last Stand: Ted Turner's Quest to Save a Troubled Planet.* New York: Rowman & Littlefield, 2013.

Williams, Sara Lockwood. *Twenty Years of Education for Journalism.* Columbia, MO: E. W. Stephens Publishing Co., 1929.

Wong, Julia Carrie. "Facebook Policy Chief Admits Hiring PR Firm to Attack George Soros." *The Guardian.* November 21, 2018. https://www.theguardian.com/technology/2018/nov/21/facebook-admits-definers-pr-george-soros-critics-sandberg-zuckerberg.

Wood, Joseph, comp. *Eighteenth Annual Report of the Maine Press Association for the Year Ending February 1, 1881.* Skowhegan, ME: Joseph Wood, 6 Madison Street, 1881.

Wood, Joseph, comp. *Nineteenth Annual Report of the Proceedings of the Maine Press Association for the Year Ending, February 1, 1882.* Bar Harbor, ME: Mount Desert Publishing Company, 1882.

Wood, Joseph, ed. *Transactions of the Maine Editors and Publishers' Association, from 1870 To 1874, Inclusive.* Wiscasset, ME: Printed by Joseph Wood, 1874.

Xuanzun, Liu. "Social Credit System Must Bankrupt Discredited People: Former Official." *Global Times.* May 20, 2018. http://www.globaltimes.cn/content/1103262.shtml.

Young, James Harvey. *American Health Quackery: Collected Essays of James Harvey Young.* Princeton, NJ: Princeton University Press, 1992.

Young, James Harvey. *Pure Food: Securing the Federal Food and Drugs Act of 1906.* Princeton, NJ: Princeton University Press, 1914.

Young, James Harvey. *The Toadstool Millionaires: A Social History of Patent Medicines in America Before Federal Regulation.* Princeton, NJ: Princeton University Press, 1961.

Zelizer, Barbie, and Stuart Allan. *Keywords in News and Journalism Studies.* New York: Open University Press, 2010.